A CONSTITUTION
FOR ALL TIMES

A CONSTITUTION FOR ALL TIMES

Pamela S. Karlan

A Boston Review Book

THE MIT PRESS Cambridge, Mass. London, England

MIT Press books may be purchased at special quantity discounts for business or sales promotional use. For information, please email special_sales@mitpress.mit.edu or write to Special Sales Department, The MIT Press, 55 Hayward Street, Cambridge, MA 02142.

This book was set in Adobe Garamond by *Boston Review* and was printed and bound in the United States of America.

Library of Congress Cataloging-in-Publication Data

Karlan, Pamela S.
A constitution for all times / Pamela S. Karlan
    pages.   cm. — (Boston review books)
ISBN 978-0-262-01989-7 (hardcover : alk. paper)
1. Constitutional law—United States 2. Political questions and judicial power. I. Title.
KF4550.K37   2013
342.73—dc23

                                    2013031529

10 9 8 7 6 5 4 3 2 1

*For Harry Blackmun, Viola Canales,
and my colleagues and students. Gladly
would I learn and gladly teach.*

CONTENTS

INTRODUCTION

IN HIS 1928 BOOK *THE PARADOXES OF LEGAL Science*, then-judge, and later Supreme Court justice, Benjamin Cardozo wrote that rather than defining "due process of law"—a critical concept in constitutional law—courts "leave it to be 'pricked out' by a process of inclusion and exclusion in individual cases. . . . It is all very well to go on pricking the lines," he observed, "but the time must come when we shall do prudently to look them over, and see whether they make a pattern or a medley of scraps and patches."

This book originated as a series of columns in *Boston Review* written between 2010 and 2013. Some of the columns addressed individual cases then pending before or recently decided by the Supreme Court.

Others covered broader questions of interpretive method or the Court's role as an institution. But taken together, they go beyond pricking the lines to lay out a coherent approach to thinking about constitutional law and the Court's role in our democracy.

The pieces, which have been updated for this book, concern several overarching themes. The first has to do with the era in which we find ourselves. Conservatives have developed a series of interpretive tools that purport to provide objective bases for judicial decisions that advance a conservative political agenda. Assertions of "originalism," "textualism," and "judicial restraint," however, have served as a smokescreen. Justice Antonin Scalia, the leading contemporary judicial exponent of textualism and originalism has repeatedly claimed that these methods make the answers to the issues that most sharply divide the court "easy." He is wrong. The cases that arrive at the Supreme Court require *judgment*, and that judgment demands serious thought about how a document originally drafted in the late eighteenth century should be understood today. During the debate over the impeachment of President Richard Nixon, the great Texas Representative Barbara Jordan, referring to the opening words of the Constitution, reminded us, "When the document was completed on the seventeenth of September 1787 I was not included in that 'We, the people'" and that it was only "through the process of amendment, interpretation and court decision" that she had "finally been included."

Justice Anthony Kennedy's opinion for the Court in *Lawrence v. Texas* (2003), the decision that struck down Texas's criminalization of consensual homosexual intimacy, confirms that this process is ongoing. The framers of our Constitution and its most important amendments, he declared,

> knew times can blind us to certain truths and later generations can see that laws once thought necessary and proper in fact serve only to oppress. As the Constitution endures, persons in every generation can invoke its principles in their own search for greater freedom.

PAMELA S. KARLAN   XI

The Constitution that is being interpreted today is simply not the same as the framers' Constitution, the Reconstruction-era Constitution, or the New Deal Constitution. Liberals and progressives must stop being defensive about our constitutional arguments. The fact that we acknowledge complexity is a strength, not a weakness, of our position.

The second theme is the complicated relationship between the Court and the democratic process. Like the two hands emerging from the sheet of paper to draw one another in M. C. Escher's famous 1948 lithograph *Drawing Hands*, the Supreme Court emerges from the political process—in the sense that the Court's membership, and thus the justices' viewpoints, are a product of broad political and intellectual movements—even as its decisions fundamentally shape the possibilities and boundaries of that political process going forward. If the Court permits restrictive voter registration practices—as it has—or strikes down restrictions on political spending—as it also has—this will influence the shape of the elections that produce the public officials who nominate and confirm future members of the Court.

The final theme is the importance of public attention to and argument about what the Constitution means. On Constitution Day 1937, President Franklin Roosevelt reminded us that the Constitution is "a layman's document, not a lawyer's contract." He spoke of "an unending struggle" between capacious and restrictive interpretations. President Roosevelt was right: that struggle continues today. Arguments over the meaning of equality, the scope of privacy in light of modern technology, and the nature of our criminal justice system are still too important to be left solely to the Supreme Court or to lawyers.

I wrote the pieces in this book to make those arguments accessible to a broader public interested in the range of issues the Constitution touches upon: civil rights and civil liberties; the power of government to deal with pressing social and economic issues; and the fair and effective functioning of the democratic process. Everyday citizens have much to say about these matters. Recall the striking moment in January 2011 when, for the first time in history, the members of the House of Representatives began the legislative session by reading nearly the entire Constitution aloud. The most moving portion occurred when Georgia Representative John Lewis read the Thirteenth Amendment, which abolished slavery. As a twenty-something civil rights activist during the 1960s, Lewis did more than any Supreme Court Justice, public official, or lawyer to realize the promise of that amendment, and his example should continue to move new generations of Americans "to form a more perfect union, establish justice, insure domestic tranquility, provide for the common defense, promote the general welfare, and secure the blessings of liberty to ourselves and our posterity," as the Constitution commits us.

In writing this book, I owe special debts to four groups of people. Deb Chasman, Josh Cohen, and Simon Waxman at *Boston Review* spurred me to write, and helped me to think through, the columns that underlie this book. My colleagues and students at Stanford Law School continually challenge and inspire me. My clients and co-counsel in the cases I have litigated at the Stanford Law School Supreme Court Litigation Clinic and in the civil rights community more generally remind me of the practical importance of constitutional interpretation and show how individual litigants with the courage of their convictions can produce constitutional change. And my collaboration with Goodwin Liu and Chris Schroeder on *Keeping Faith With the Constitution* is a foundation of my approach to constitutional law. My partner Viola Canales remains hors catégorie.

Part I

*Originalism, Activism,
and Constitutional Values*

1. In the Beginning

SINCE 1789, CONSTITUTIONS WORLDWIDE HAVE come and gone. According to University of Chicago Law professor Tom Ginsburg, the median lifespan of a national constitution is eight years—roughly the life expectancy of a Great Dane. Why has the U.S. Constitution endured?

Not because it is unchanged. The Constitution has been reshaped by formal amendments, Supreme Court decisions, and shifting popular understandings of such broad terms as "commerce" and "equal protection." Although the original text largely remains, fidelity to the Constitution requires reading its words in light of the principles they express: principles embracing liberty, equality, and opportunity, as well as a government powerful enough to address pressing national issues and constrained enough to prevent tyranny. Moreover, fidelity requires bringing those principles to bear on fresh problems—interpreting the Constitution, as Justice Oliver Wendell Holmes said, in light of "what this country has become."

The framers could not have imagined the Environmental Protection Agency or the Americans with Disabilities Act, the Internet or genetic testing. They restricted the franchise to white male property owners. And they punished private, consensual sexual activity. But none of this settles what the Constitution now permits or prohibits or demands. Working that out requires that we ask how the Constitution's text and animating principles should be understood *today*. While explaining why the Eighth Amendment's prohibition on cruel and unusual punishments forbids imposing on juveniles life sentences with no possibility of parole, Justice John Paul Stevens powerfully observed:

Society changes. Knowledge accumulates. We learn, sometimes, from our mistakes. Punishments that did not seem cruel and unusual at one time may, in the light of reason and experience, be found cruel and unusual at a later time.

To take a "static approach to the law," he warned, risks leading us "to abandon the moral commitment embodied in the Eighth Amendment."

This common sense idea that constitutional interpretation demands an interplay between animating principles and changing circumstances lies at the heart of the Court's most celebrated opinion: *Brown v. Board of Education* (1954). In *Brown* a unanimous Court decided that the Fourteenth Amendment's equal protection clause condemns racially segregated schools. But the Congress that had proposed the Fourteenth Amendment had segregated both the public galleries from which citizens watched the debate and the public schools it controlled.

When the Court decided *Brown*, it refused to "turn the clock back to 1868 when the Amendment was adopted, or even to 1896" when, in *Plessy v. Ferguson*, the Court upheld the segregation of railroad cars against constitutional attack. The Court of 1954 decisively rejected the idea that the country should be ruled by the understanding of the Fourteenth Amendment held by those who adopted it. Instead, the Court declared, the country "must consider public education in the light of its full development and its present place in American life throughout the Nation." Nearly a century's experience with *de jure* segregation had proved that, when it came to race, "separate but equal" violated equal protection of the laws.

Similarly, the framers may have thought that the power of Congress to "regulate Commerce" involved only trade in goods and not their manufacture. But in the face of an integrated national economy, this understanding gave way to a more expansive conception of commerce that empowered the federal government to regulate minimum wages and occupational safety.

Most profoundly, the Bill of Rights did not originally protect Americans against state or local governments. Through a process known as "incorporation," the Fourteenth Amendment's due process clause has become a conduit by which Americans have gained such protections. Change took time: after the ratification of the Fourteenth Amendment, nearly a century passed before most of the protections we now consider fundamental—including freedom of speech and religion and the right to trial by jury in criminal cases—were applied fully to the states.

Unfortunately, in recent years, the debate about constitutional interpretation has been dominated by a slippery and misleading "originalism" that claims to reject the concept of the Constitution as a changing document. Despite its connotations, originalism is a recent phenomenon. It began in Reagan-era attacks on the Warren Court. Then-Attorney General Edwin Meese proposed "a Jurisprudence of Original Intention": What would the framers do if they were asked the question we face today?

Asking what James Madison would do sounds like a good way to prevent judges from overriding democratically enacted laws. But even conservatives soon abandoned this original originalism—perhaps because it was impossible to figure out how our forebears would answer questions they could not even formulate; perhaps because the answers were unpalatable. It would, for example, require a vivid imagination to argue that the authors of the Fourteenth Amendment would have cared at all about sex discrimination, especially because they enshrined it in the Amendment itself (in the reduction-of-representation clause of Section 2).

Rejecting "original intent" as their touchstone, originalists shifted to "original public meaning." Justice Scalia, for example, says that we are bound by the Constitution's words as they were understood by "ordinary citizens in the founding generation." This move to original public meaning, however, does nothing to change the unpalatable answers: ordinary citizens in 1868 did not think that "equal protection of the laws" condemned segregated schools or forbade sex discrimination in government employment.

Moreover, originalists drop their originalism when their own principles push in a different direction. Consider Justice Scalia's opinion in *Kyllo v. United States* (2001). In that case, police, while standing on public property, used a thermal-imaging device to determine that Danny Lee Kyllo was consuming huge amounts of energy in order to grow marijuana in the basement of his home. Justice Scalia interpreted the word "search" in the Fourth Amendment's ban on "unreasonable search and seizure" to encompass the thermal imaging technique. In 1789 a search would have required some physical intrusion onto private property. Still, Justice Scalia relied on a general principle of privacy to conclude that the Constitution protects what goes on inside a house. And Justice Scalia took a similar approach in *District of Columbia v. Heller* (2008), discussed in the next chapter, when he used the Second Amendment as the basis for striking down Washington D.C.'s handgun ban.

Originalism offers the false hope of a principled constraint on judicial power. It is a good thing originalism is a new invention, and rarely followed: if judges had hewed to the contemporary forms of originalist argument throughout American history, the Constitution would never have lasted. More fundamentally, when today's professed originalists abandon that position in service of constitutional principles, rather than hurling back at them the meaningless accusation of judicial activism, we should press the real argument: the most important constitutional principles require liberty, equality, and opportunity for all.

2. Founding Firearms

THE IDEA THAT THE MEANING OF A CONSTI-
tutional provision is frozen at the moment of its
ratification—and that its meaning can be discerned
and applied to contemporary controversies in an in-
contestable manner—lies at the heart of arguments
for originalism, an interpretive method Justice Scalia
has spent his career championing.

But both judicial and popular conceptions of
constitutional meaning undeniably change over
time, and there is often disagreement over how to
understand the historical evidence. Ironically nothing
illustrates this more powerfully than the recent
history of the Second Amendment—the subject of
Justice Scalia's most avowedly originalist opinion for

the Court and an issue very much on the minds of both Congress and the people in the wake of recent tragic shootings from Connecticut to Arizona and in between. Gun control proposals in the Senate following the mass killing in Newtown foundered in part over concerns that expanded background checks and other restrictions would breach protections supposedly enshrined in the Constitution.

Yet in 1991 former Chief Justice Warren Burger called the claim that the Constitution protects an individual's right to possess a handgun "one of the greatest pieces of fraud—I repeat the word 'fraud'— on the American public by special interest groups that I have ever seen in my lifetime." Chief Justice Burger embraced what had been the consensus view among federal courts throughout the 20th century: when the framers wrote, "A well regulated Militia, being necessary to the security of a free State, the right of the people to keep and bear Arms, shall not be infringed," they were protecting the ability of individuals to participate in organized state militias.

Thus, for example, in *United States v. Miller* (1939), the Supreme Court rejected two defendants' claims that the Amendment protected their right to possess a sawed-off shotgun. The Court found no evidence that owning such a gun "has some reasonable relationship to the preservation or efficiency of a well regulated militia."

But Justice Scalia's opinion for the Court in *District of Columbia v. Heller* (2008) adopted a very different view of the Second Amendment, holding that it "protects an individual right to possess a firearm unconnected with service in a militia." The decision reflected a dramatic shift in constitutional understanding.

So what changed between 1991 and 2008? Clearly not the words of the Second Amendment. Nor did historians discover some previously unknown 18th-century documentation of the amendment's meaning. To be sure, during the intervening years some legal and historical scholarship had advanced arguments for an individual-rights, rather than a collective-rights, approach. But many leading historians of the period continue to adhere to a collective-rights interpretation. And as legal scholars such as Adam Winkler, in his magisterial 2011 book *Gunfight*, and Reva Siegel have shown, the triumph of the individual-rights approach in *Heller* is part of a larger story of cultural change and political struggle that simultaneously transformed popular understandings, scholarship, and the membership of the Court.

That being said, what divided the Court in *Heller* was not primarily interpretive method. Both Justice Scalia and the dissenters in the 5-4 decision devoted a great deal of attention to textual exegesis and historical inquiry. Instead where they differed was over the meaning of "keep and bear Arms" and the significance of the first thirteen words of the amendment referring to the "well regulated Militia." The majority saw those words as "prefatory" and focused on what it called the "operative" language announcing a right. By contrast, Justice Stevens's dissent treated the militia discussion as "preamble" shaping and constraining what came after.

Despite relying on similar sources—such as the drafting and ratification histories of the amendment, the history of contemporaneous state constitutional provisions, and existing practice at the time the amendment was ratified—the majority and the dissent reached divergent conclusions about the amendment's original meaning. Arguments about that meaning proved indeterminate. In particular, Justice Stephen Breyer's dissent detailed various restrictions on firearms that existed during the colonial period and concluded, "Irrespective of what the Framers could have thought, we know what they did think"—that restrictions on firearms were consistent with the Second Amendment.

When Justice Scalia turned from abstract principle to actually resolving the case before him, he abandoned originalism in favor of the kind of contemporary understanding he so often decries. Why does the Second Amendment protect the ownership of handguns, a form of "Arms" quite different from the muskets and rifles owned by colonial Americans?

Justice Scalia responded that it "border[ed] on the frivolous" to suggest that the amendment protected only 18th-century weapons: "We do not interpret constitutional rights that way." Citing cases involving First Amendment protection of online speech and Fourth Amendment protection against the government's use of thermal-imaging devices, Justice Scalia explained, the "Second Amendment extends, prima facie, to all instruments that constitute bearable arms, even those that were not in existence at the time of the founding."

Justice Scalia's reading is only plausible because the Court sees the words of the amendment as standing for a broader principle about the right to self-defense using available technology. But if "Arms" should be construed at a level of abstraction that takes into account contemporary understandings—and Justice Scalia found constitutional relevance in the fact that handguns are "overwhelmingly chosen by American society" today for purposes of self-defense—then why do originalists look to 18th- or 19th-century understandings to determine the scope of terms such as "liberty," "cruel and unusual punishment," or "equal protection of the laws"?

Moreover, modern practice also shaped the Court's understanding of which "Arms" the Amendment protects. According to *Heller* handguns are protected, but sawed-off shotguns and military-grade weapons such as machine guns are not. As Winkler points out, the Court could exclude these weapons as "dangerous and unusual" precisely because existing gun-control laws have effectively criminalized their possession. "Rather than defer to the original understanding, the majority opinion looks to contemporary government regulation," Winkler writes. "This sounds a lot like a right evolving with the times—that is, a living Constitution."

There also is little originalism in the Court's treatment of the regulations themselves. Having announced an individual right to "keep and bear" handguns, the Court then indicated its receptivity to a broad range of government regulations, including laws "forbidding the carrying of firearms in sensitive places such as schools and government buildings" and blanket bans on gun possession by felons and mentally ill persons. That receptivity is inconsistent with the Court's equation of the "right of the people" set forth in the Second Amendment with the rights protected by the First and Fourth Amendments. After all, the Court has repeatedly protected free speech inside schools and other government buildings, and mentally ill people retain protection against unreasonable searches and seizures.

Here, too, the explanation for the Court's position lies not in the 18th or 19th centuries, but in the 21st. In *Heller* the Court signaled its approval of these restrictions because, whether the justices admit it or not, they care about consequences. They engage in interest balancing: governments are entitled to conclude that the social costs of permitting weapons in schools or government buildings outweigh any individual right. Even after *Heller*, the Court has let stand lower-court decisions upholding restrictions on the right to carry concealed weapons outside the home. The difference on this point between the majority and Justice Breyer is not that one engages in interest balancing and the other does not. Rather it lies in Justice Breyer's candor and the majority's disingenuousness, and in how they weigh the competing considerations.

While *Heller* changed the doctrinal landscape, its effect on the scope of permissible legislation is fairly small. Standing alone, *Heller* held only that governments cannot enact absolute bans on handgun possession among law-abiding individuals for self-defense within their own homes. But that is not to say that the decision was insignificant, for by articulating a constitutional right, the Court can shift the nature of the political debate by reinforcing gun-control opponents' claims that there is something constitutionally suspect about restrictions on weapons. And in that way, the justices may influence the future evolution of legal regulation just as they were themselves influenced by previous evolutions of political and popular understandings.

3. Why Interpretive Methods Matter

DURING THE SUPREME COURT'S 2010 TERM, IN the course of oral argument over the constitutionality under the First Amendment of a California law that restricted the sale of violent video games to minors, Justice Samuel Alito got a big laugh from the audience when he interjected, "What Justice Scalia wants to know is what James Madison thought about video games."

Of course Madison had no such thoughts, but the question perfectly captures the challenge that new technologies present to originalism—the theory that, when adjudicating constitutional questions, judges should rely essentially on how constitutional provisions were understood at the time of their enactment.

The Supreme Court is frequently called on to apply the Constitution to situations the framers could never have dreamed of. And when it comes to the Constitution, technology can cut in both directions. Sometimes, a new technology fits relatively easily into existing notions of constitutional protection, as it did in the video games case. Justice Scalia's opinion for the Court holds that video games qualify for First Amendment protection because they are a form of expression that communicates ideas, in part "through features distinctive to the medium." Citing the Court's decision in *Burstyn v. Wilson* (1952), which reached a similar conclusion with regard to movies, Justice Scalia reminds us, "Whatever the challenges of applying the Constitution to ever-advancing technology, 'the basic principles of freedom of speech and the press . . . do not vary' when a new and different medium for communication appears."

At other times, as with *United States v. Jones* (2012), the use of new technologies poses important challenges to traditional understandings of constitutional protections. *Jones* involved the government's covert placement of a GPS device on the undercarriage of a car owned by Antoine Jones, a nightclub proprietor in Washington, D.C. Police suspected Jones of distributing cocaine, and the device provided them a record of the car's location and movement, every ten seconds for a month. At Jones's trial, the prosecution used the record as evidence that his car had repeatedly traveled to a suspected "stash house" where large amounts of narcotics had been found. Jones's counsel argued that the GPS data should not have been admitted at his trial. The Court had to decide whether attaching a GPS device and gathering information from it constituted a "search" or "seizure" within the meaning of the Fourth Amendment, which prohibits "unreasonable searches and seizures." If using the GPS device amounted to search or seizure, then the government needed a valid warrant, which it did not have.

The Supreme Court held unanimously that the government had searched Jones's car. But the justices offered three separate opinions explaining why that was so. These illustrate the complexity both of the specific questions—whether and how the Constitution restricts the government's use of GPS devices—and of constitutional interpretation generally. And they show why a judge's interpretive method matters.

Justice Scalia's opinion for the Court (joined by Chief Justice John Roberts and Justices Kennedy, Clarence Thomas, and Sonia Sotomayor), held that the act of attaching a GPS device to a car and using it to monitor the car's movements constitutes a search under the Fourth Amendment. His analysis is largely originalist: by putting the device on the car, the government physically intruded onto Jones's personal property, and this kind of trespass would have been understood, in the 18th century, as a search.

While this sort of argument might seem tempting, linking constitutional protections to traditional—physical—notions of property misses three critical points about the digital age.

First, informational privacy is becoming as vital as physical privacy. The problem in Jones's case is not that the GPS intruded a fraction of an inch into the chassis of the car; it's that the GPS provided a bounty of information about his life. The Court tackled a similar problem in *Kyllo v. United States* (2001). The decision held that police use of a thermal imaging device across the street from a suspect's home constituted a search. No one worried that the device was somehow "stealing" the heat that emanated from the house, but the justices did care that the device was capable of revealing intimate details about a target's life—the kinds of details the Fourth Amendment is intended to keep private. Justice Scalia's charmingly old-fashioned example of such protected details was the hour at which "the lady of the house takes her daily sauna and bath."

Second, the information individuals want to keep private is, more and more often, in the hands of third parties. Protecting a person's physical property does nothing to safeguard these data. Cases involving the Stored Communications Act—which allows federal prosecutors to access cell phone records with a lesser evidentiary showing than is required for conventional warrants—are working their way through the courts. In late 2011, a federal judge in Texas held that the Act's standard for disclosure "is below that required for the Constitution." Earlier, a federal court of appeals held similarly with regard to email.

Third, a constitutional doctrine that depends on a physical intrusion onto a target's tangible property is likely to be overtaken by technological developments. Privacy was traditionally protected as much by practical constraints as by legal principles: the sheer cost of round-the-clock surveillance by teams of law enforcement agents meant that few people faced a realistic risk of being targeted. GPS slashes those costs to pennies a day. And because software can rapidly sift through the reams of data a GPS device produces, the new technology enables pervasive government monitoring. If the government can conduct this monitoring by using drones, rather than affixing devices directly to cars, then the doctrine announced by Justice Scalia has no traction. Even more broadly, the 18th-century trespass doctrine has nothing to say about whether the government could install GPS devices on license plates before issuing them, in which case the government would not have committed a trespass as that term was understood at the time the Fourth Amendment was ratified.

Justice Alito (joined by Justices Breyer, Ruth Bader Ginsburg, and Elena Kagan) concurred in the judgment—namely, that Jones had been subjected to a search—but strongly disagreed with Justice Scalia's reasoning. Instead of grounding analysis of a "21st-century surveillance technique" in "18th-century tort law," Justice Alito relied on the framework laid out by the Court in its 1967 decision in *Katz v. United States*: Does the government's conduct violate "reasonable expectations of privacy"? Justice Alito's analysis is flexible: it recognizes that society's expectations can morph over time in response to changes in technology and social understandings. He sees that modern technology undermines the practical constraints that traditionally protected privacy, as I argue.

Thus, for him, the long-term nature of the surveillance creates the Fourth Amendment problem. "Relatively short-term monitoring of a person's movements on public streets," presumably even when it involves a GPS device, is acceptable to Justice Alito and the three justices who joined his concurrence. His approach therefore provides a different sort of protection than Justice Scalia's, but not necessarily greater protection.

If a generation raised on social media and ubiquitous smart phones draws a different line between what counts as private and what doesn't, then Justice Alito's doctrine will come to reflect that new, perhaps less protective, line. If individuals become used to the idea that their private information is shared with vast networks of people and corporations, they may become less able to protect that information from the government's gaze as well.

Justice Sotomayor homed in on this point in her separate concurring opinion. (She also joined Justice Scalia's opinion for the Court.) Justice Sotomayor staked out the approach most concerned with protecting privacy. In cases involving "novel modes of surveillance that do not depend upon a physical invasion on property," she observed, "the majority opinion's trespassory test may provide little guidance." She notes that even short-term GPS monitoring could provide the government with "a wealth of detail about [a person's] familial, political, professional, religious, and sexual associations," which could be aggregated and mined years down the road, perhaps inhibiting the exercise of fundamental associational and expressive freedoms. And she expressed a willingness "to reconsider the premise"—long relied upon by the Court—"that an individual has no reasonable expectation of privacy in information voluntarily disclosed to third parties." If the Court were to follow her lead here, it would be more difficult for the government to gain access to individuals' phone and bank records held by businesses.

In many ways, the decision in *Jones* was a victory for Fourth Amendment values: had the case been decided in the government's favor, it would have been a disaster. But the ruling left open a host of important questions as well. Some are technical: Does the use of a GPS device invariably require a warrant based on a neutral magistrate's finding of probable cause, or would some lesser standard, such as reasonable suspicion, suffice? Others are more fundamental. We are left wondering how we should understand privacy in an electronic age. In future cases, the Court will confront a series of related issues. Already the lower federal and state courts are deeply divided about whether, for example, existing doctrine that allows police to search anyone they have arrested also permits them to search a detained person's smart phone.

The foundation of modern Fourth Amendment law, in many respects, is Justice Louis Brandeis's dissent in *Olmstead v. United States* (1928). In explaining why wiretaps, even though they involved no trespass into the target's home, should be treated as a search, Justice Brandeis quoted the Court in *Weems v. United States* (1910):

Time works changes, brings into existence new conditions and purposes. Therefore a principle, to be vital, must be capable of wider application than the mischief which gave it birth. This is peculiarly true of constitutions.

And it is especially true of how we should understand the Fourth Amendment today.

4. What Do We Mean By Judicial Activism?

A WEAK ECONOMIC RECOVERY. THE AIRWAVES filled with demagoguery about important constitutional issues. A president who chides the Supreme Court for striking down a major piece of federal reform legislation. And, in response to charges of a pro-corporate tilt on a Court with a narrow conservative majority, Justice Roberts defends the Court's intervention with the claim that judges do nothing more than "lay the article of the Constitution which is invoked beside the statute which is challenged" in order "to decide whether the latter squares with the former."

2013? No, 1936. That mechanistic image of the judicial process was the handiwork of Justice *Owen*

Roberts, responding to critics who complained that the Court was overriding New Deal economic legislation on the basis of its own political preferences. Current Chief Justice John Roberts seeks to deflect parallel charges of judicial activism—the idea that judges improperly strike down democratically enacted laws according to their own moral and political convictions—by appealing to the metaphor of an umpire calling balls and strikes.

Indeed, the phrase "judicial activist" (or "activist judge") is so frequently used that it has come to exemplify what George Orwell described in "Politics and the English Language" as a term with "no meaning except in so far as it signifies 'something not desirable.'" Consider how it has been employed in recent judicial confirmation hearings. During the confirmation hearings for Justice Sotomayor, conservative senators who worried that she would be a judicial activist pointed to her appeals court decision in *Ricci v. DeStefano* (2009), in which she had *refused* to override employment policies adopted by the democratically elected government of New Haven. A year later the National Rifle Association announced that it would oppose Justice Kagan's nomination because she might not be activist enough—her record suggested to them that she would uphold laws restricting gun possession. Meanwhile, liberal senators spent the same hearings excoriating the activism of the conservatives on the Court, who had voted in *Citizens United v. Federal Election Commission* (2010) to strike down certain federal restrictions on corporate involvement in the election process.

The consensus that judges must refrain from imposing their personal beliefs goes back at least to Alexander Hamilton's *Federalist No. 78*. Hamilton described the judiciary as the "least dangerous" branch because it

> has no influence over either the sword or the purse; no direction either of the strength or of the wealth of the society; and can take no active resolution whatever. It may truly be said to have neither FORCE nor WILL,

but merely judgment; and must ultimately depend upon the aid of the executive arm even for the efficacy of its judgments.

We expect judges to be impartial and independent. That is why federal judges have life tenure. But we also demand that they respect democratic choices. They should enforce the policy decisions of the political branches—local and federal—unless the Constitution commands otherwise.

It's that "unless" that causes the difficulty. The Constitution is the "supreme Law of the Land." So, faced with a federal, state, or local law or policy that violates the Constitution, a judge must act. Judges would violate their oaths of office if, for example, they sat back and allowed the government to put people in jail for engaging in constitutionally protected activity (remember how the Commonwealth of Virginia threatened Mildred and Richard Loving with imprisonment for marrying across racial lines?) or permitted local officials to adopt policies that undermined the federal government's exercise of its constitutional authority (think about Arizona's attempt to adopt its own immigration policy). At the same time, judges equally violate their oaths of office if they strike down properly enacted laws because they think those laws are unwise or contravene the judges' personal moral or religious codes.

The consequences of bold judicial action can be awful. In *Dred Scott v. Sandford* (1857), for example, after the Court declared that black people could never be considered citizens it struck down Congress's ban on slavery north of the 36th parallel as an unconstitutional denial of slaveholders' property rights. This was one of the lowest points in the Court's history.

That said, some of the Court's greatest triumphs involved major intervention: "one person, one vote," now a bedrock constitutional principle, was judicially imposed on the nation 50 years ago by a set of decisions rightly called the "reapportionment revolution." And some of the Court's greatest mistakes came when it showed timidity. Consider the decisions in *Plessy v.*

Ferguson (1896) and *Giles v. Harris* (1903), in which the Court's passivity before, respectively, Louisiana's segregation ordinance and Alabama's disenfranchisement statute gave the green light to Jim Crow laws. To riff on Barry Goldwater, vigor in the protection of constitutional rights is no vice; restraint in the face of constitutional violations is no virtue.

These days, when it comes to accusations of judicial activism, the favored conservative target is the Warren Court (1953–1969). Yet most of its decisions declaring laws unconstitutional were not directed at Congress, but rather at state and local policies—the South's adherence to Jim Crow; Connecticut's refusal to allow married couples to use contraceptives; Florida's refusal to provide lawyers to indigent defendants—that departed from a national consensus about constitutional guarantees of liberty and due process. By contrast the Rehnquist and Roberts Courts have struck down more acts of Congress per year than any other Courts in our history. And the most trigger-happy justices have been conservatives.

The question is not *whether* federal judges should strike down popularly enacted policies but *when*. This question has no mechanical answer. So let's drop the vacuous accusations of activism and instead argue about the right answers to constitutional questions, and the real meaning of fidelity to the most important constitutional principles: liberty, equality, democracy, and opportunity for all.

And when we have that discussion, let's bear in mind that obligations of constitutional fidelity do not stop at the bench. The Constitution requires that all public officials—federal, state, and local; judicial, executive, and legislative—take an oath to support the Constitution. But many fail to take that oath seriously, and laws and policies are adopted out of political expediency by legislators who know that the courts will strike them down. Thus Senator Arlen Specter, for instance, voted in favor of the Military Commissions Act, which sharply limited the right of Guantánamo detainees to challenge their continued confinement, and then turned around and urged the Supreme Court to strike the Act down, calling it "anathema" to what he acknowledged as "fundamental" constitutional guarantees of liberty. Similarly, local legislators have passed ordinances denying undocumented immigrants the right to live or work in their communities, despite the fact that the Constitution clearly grants control over immigration to the federal government. And the repeated history of states passing restrictive abortion laws that cannot possibly survive judicial review reflects the worst form of political grandstanding.

Politicians have constitutional responsibilities, too. And if they showed more restraint, judges would not have to intervene so often.

5. The Unhealthy Activism of the Roberts Court

THE PATIENT PROTECTION AND AFFORDABLE Care Act—a.k.a. Obamacare—is one of the most momentous pieces of federal legislation of the last half-century. But ironically the opponents who launched the failed constitutional attack on the Act used its modesty as the basis for their challenge.

If Congress had voted to provide every American with health care through a national health service, that law would have been almost immune from constitutional challenge. It has long been understood that the power to tax and spend—enumerated in Article I of the Constitution—lies largely with Congress: it decides what to tax and how to spend the revenue. To be sure, those powers are limited, but the limits come from other constitutional provisions—for example, the First Amendment would prohibit Congress from imposing a special tax on atheists or providing better benefits to registered Republicans—and, most importantly, from our democratic system, which gives voters the power to eject from office those representatives who support objectionable policies.

So why did the Act come within a hair's breadth of being struck down, saved by a 5-4 Supreme Court decision that saw Chief Justice Roberts join the Court's moderate wing? The answer lies in an argument advanced by libertarians and conservatives who sought a return to pre-New Deal interpretation of the commerce clause. That clause gives Congress the power to "regulate Commerce . . . among the several States." Although the 19th-century Supreme Court drew a sharp line between commerce and other aspects of the economy—such as agriculture and manufacturing—by the mid-20th century, the Court had recognized reality. As Justice Robert Jackson put it:

> Questions of the power of Congress are not to be decided by reference to any formula which would give controlling force to nomenclature such as 'production' ... and foreclose consideration of the actual effects of the activity in question upon interstate commerce.

That statement came in the Court's unanimous 1942 decision in *Wickard v. Filburn*. There, a farmer challenged a federal penalty for growing and then consuming on his farm more wheat than a federal marketing order had permitted him. (The controls on wheat supply were part of a price-support program intended to help farmers during the Great Depression.) Filburn argued that the commerce power did not permit Congress to regulate his at-home consumption because his activities were purely local, thus not part of interstate commerce. Justice Jackson rejected that contention, writing that Filburn's grain "supplies a need of the man who grew it which would otherwise be reflected by purchases in the open market.

Home-grown wheat in this sense competes with wheat in commerce." He pointed out that the effect of Filburn's decision on interstate commerce, "taken together with that of many others similarly situated, is far from trivial."

Since *Wickard v. Filburn*, the Court has deferred to congressional judgments about the scope of the commerce power. That deference sustained, among other things, the public-accommodations provisions of the Civil Rights Act of 1964, one of the cornerstones of modern antidiscrimination law. Nearly all modern federal labor and consumer-rights legislation depends on this expansive understanding of the commerce power. And although the Rehnquist Court later struck down two federal statutes on the grounds that the activities they regulated (possessing a gun near a school and committing gender-motivated violence) were non-commercial, it reaffirmed the proposition that Congress can regulate all essentially economic activity. Its 2005 decision in *Gonzales v. Raich*, for example, upheld Congress's power to criminalize the personal cultivation and possession of marijuana for medical use. Justice Stevens's opinion explained that Congress had enacted comprehensive national drug laws and found "no difficulty concluding that Congress had a rational basis for believing that failure to regulate the intrastate manufacture and possession of marijuana would leave a gaping hole" in that regulatory regime. And both he and Justice Scalia in his concurring opinion also relied on the Necessary and Proper Clause of Article I, which authorizes Congress "to make all Laws which shall be necessary and proper for carrying into Execution" its enumerated powers.

The argument for the constitutionality of the individual mandate as a permissible regulation of commerce flowed easily from *Wickard* and *Raich*. Health care constitutes more than 17 percent of U.S. GDP. And since the 1940s, the Court has recognized that insurance companies engage in interstate commerce. The Affordable Care Act is a comprehensive regulation and reform of health care that, among other things, forbids insurance companies from denying coverage on the basis of preexisting conditions or from imposing lifetime caps on benefits. Congress concluded that aspects of the Act would be undercut if individuals could refuse to purchase insurance until they needed care. Thus the mandate. Moreover, Congress concluded that broadening the insurance pool to include healthy individuals would help to lower insurance premiums and administrative costs.

Maybe Congress was wrong about these empirical judgments. I don't know; I'm just a law professor. But the constitutional question was not whether Congress's judgment was *correct*; rather, it was whether Congress's judgment was rational. In this regard, the many prizewinning economists who agree with Congress are enough to justify its decision.

And yet the Supreme Court held that the law lay outside the commerce power. (A different majority, also 5-4, upheld the law on the alternative ground that because the individual mandate in fact only required individuals without health insurance to pay an additional tax, it could be sustained as a permissible exercise of Congress's taxing power.) The five Justices who thought Congress had gone beyond its commerce power saw a constitutionally significant difference between the individual mandate and all prior law: the mandate, they argued, regulates inactivity—the refusal to buy insurance—rather than something people are already doing, such as growing wheat or marijuana.

But this argument assumes a bright line where reality is more complicated. Virtually everyone will spend money on health care during their lifetimes. That spending itself is clearly economic activity within Congress's reach. What the individual mandate does is regulate the timing of that activity, in essence requiring people to pay upfront as part of a pool rather than gamble that they will be able to pay when the services are needed or that society will pay for the services if they can't.

Moreover, in exercising other enumerated powers—such as running the court system or providing for the national defense—Congress has long required individuals to engage in activities they might otherwise choose not to perform. Jury service and registration for the draft are the two most familiar examples, but for those opponents of the individual mandate who want to return to the time of the Framers, here's another: the Militia Act of 1792 required white men between the ages of eighteen and 45 to provide themselves with muskets and other equipment. Because the national welfare required it, Congress required individuals to purchase goods from the market. Other laws operating today also penalize the refusal to engage in economic activity. Both the Sherman Antitrust Act and federal labor law, for example, prohibit certain kinds of boycotts.

The architects of the commerce challenge that nearly succeeded trained their sights not on the activity/inactivity distinction but on the entire edifice of modern regulatory law. In this view, the Court went off track when it abandoned the divide between commerce and other forms of economic activity. If this roll-back-the-twentieth-century attack were to succeed, health-care reform would be only the first statute to fall. Federal safety standards; anti-discrimination provisions; minimum-wage and hour laws for agricultural workers, miners, and factory workers; and most other efforts to protect employees from the power of owners would go too, since those employees are not engaged in commerce in its narrowest sense. As Justices Scalia, Kennedy, Thomas, and Alito gratuitously observed in their joint dissent:

> We now have sizable federal Departments devoted to subjects not mentioned among Congress' enumerated powers, and only marginally related to commerce: the Department of Education, the Department of Health and Human Services, the Department of Housing and Urban Development.

In taking this pot shot, the dissenters ignored not only the way that these departments *are* related to commerce—a huge share of the nation's economy involves the areas these agencies address—but more profoundly the ways in which these departments vindicate Fourteenth Amendment–based liberty and equality rights by ensuring access to education, health care, and affordable housing.

In the short run, it's unclear whether the Court's decision in the *Affordable Care Act Cases* will have repercussions with respect to other commerce clause–based legislation. But if it does, then the Court's decision—and not the 2010 health care reform— would mean victory for a genuinely radical program.

Part II

*The Supreme Court
and the Democratic Process*

6. The Long Shadow of *Bush v. Gore*

It is one of the unforgettable moments in recent Supreme Court history, and a decision that will endure in the nation's memory: in *Bush v. Gore* (2000), the Court stepped in to decide the presidential election. The Court halted Florida's recount and announced that the state's method of reviewing ballots violated the equal protection clause of the Fourteenth Amendment.

Although the justices had found a constitutional violation, they weren't interested—as the Court's unsigned opinion made clear—in vindicating equality more broadly. Their decision, the justices wrote, "is limited to the present circumstances, for the problem of equal protection in election processes generally presents many complexities." Indeed, *Bush v. Gore* has been cited by the members of the Court only once—and then in the middle of a footnote in a solo dissent by Justice Thomas advancing the truly radical suggestion that Congress lacks any authority to regulate the presidential election.

The Court's interest in leveling the political playing field waned as quickly as it waxed. Since *Bush v. Gore*, the Court has consistently refused opportunities to make the electoral process fairer. Consider gerrymandering: nothing makes ballots more worthless than having the election results foreordained by sitting politicians' artful jiggering of the district lines. Yet the Supreme Court has refused to do anything about the increasingly aggressive and sophisticated means by which officeholders pick their constituents rather than the other way around.

Moreover, the Court has turned a purported concern with voter chicanery into a green light for draconian voter-identification laws, despite virtually no evidence of voting fraud perpetrated through impersonation of registered voters at the polls. The Court also has gutted the Voting Rights Act— Congress's most notable and successful attempt to promote equality within the political process. By striking down Section 4 of the Act, the Court effectively eliminated the requirement that jurisdictions with a history of discriminatory election laws obtain federal approval before implementing new policies. And most notoriously, the Court has dismissed the very idea that equalizing chances for political influence is a legitimate value when it comes to campaign-finance regulation.

But *Bush v. Gore* casts a shadow far beyond the Court's election-law docket. At the time of the decision, many observers—including Justices Ginsburg, Breyer, and Stevens in dissent—warned that the Court might lose the nation's confidence in its role as an impartial guardian of the law. That didn't happen immediately, although by June 2012 a majority of respondents to a poll carried out by the Alliance for Justice expressed concern that "the Supreme Court makes decisions based on a political agenda instead of the law." A May 2012 Pew survey found that public approval of the Supreme Court was at its lowest point in 25 years. But whatever the effect on public confidence, the Court apparently gained a disturbing degree of confidence in itself. Having decided in 2000 that Congress could not be trusted to have the final word in the presidential election—even though the Twelfth Amendment establishes Congress, not the Supreme Court, as the ultimate arbiter—a number of justices have made a habit of expressing their distrust for Congress in other areas.

There has seldom been a Court so sure of itself relative to the political branches of the federal government. Perhaps that comes from the narrowness of the justices' experience with those branches. In contrast to the Court that decided *Brown v. Board of Education*—which boasted a former governor, several former members of Congress, and a number of high executive-branch officials—today's Court is far less diverse when it comes to government experience (even if it is more diverse with respect to race and gender). Not a single member of the current Court has been elected to public office. Before Justice Kagan's appointment, every sitting justice had come directly from a federal court of appeals. John Roberts, the current chief justice, likes it that way. In 2009 he claimed this judicial background meant the Court's "method of analysis and argument [has] shifted to the more solid grounds of legal arguments" and away from "a policy perspective." And yet the Justices continue to make assertions in their opinions about the policy effects of their decisions.

The longest-term effect of *Bush v. Gore* may actually be on the composition of the Court itself. President George W. Bush made two appointments to the Court: one when Chief Justice William Rehnquist died and another when Justice Sandra Day O'Connor retired. If his two picks—Chief Justice Roberts and Justice Alito—remain on the Court until they are the age of Justice Stevens when he retired in 2010, they will each be serving until the 2040s. No other legacy of the Bush years—save, perhaps, our staggering national debt and the war on terrorism—is likely to be so enduring.

To get a sense of how transformative those appointments already have been, we need only look at some of the cases where the substitution of Justice Alito for Justice O'Connor may have changed the bottom line.

Abortion. In 2000 the Supreme Court, by a 5-4 vote with Justice O'Connor in the majority, struck down a Nebraska statute that barred particular abortion procedures. The Court held that the law failed to include a required exception permitting the procedures when necessary to preserve a woman's health. In 2007 the Court upheld a nearly identical federal statute, again by a 5-4 vote. Challenges to a series of additional state-level restrictions on abortion are now wending their way through the lower federal courts, where proponents of the restrictions seek to rely on the 2007 opinion.

Campaign-finance regulation. In 2003 Justice O'Connor joined a 5-4 majority to uphold the

McCain-Feingold campaign-finance law against a constitutional challenge. In 2010, again by a 5-4 vote, the Court struck down parts of the law in *Citizens United v. Federal Elections Commission*, a sweeping decision that threw out a longstanding ban on independent electioneering expenditures by corporations.

Racial integration. In 2003 Justice O'Connor wrote the Court's opinion in a 5-4 decision upholding the efforts of public educational institutions (in that case, the University of Michigan Law School) to create diverse student bodies by considering race in admissions decisions. In 2007 the Court struck down decisions of popularly elected school boards in Seattle and Louisville, which sought to integrate public schools by accounting for race in pupil assignments. The vote was 5-4. Similarly, in *Fisher v. University of Texas* (2013), the Supreme Court, again by a 5-4 vote, tightened up the test Justice O'Connor had announced in the Michigan case, virtually guaranteeing a new set of challenges to affirmative action in higher education.

Sex discrimination in employment. In 1987 Justice O'Connor (the first woman to hold the job of Supreme Court Justice) was in the majority in a 6-3 decision upholding an affirmative action plan designed to give women access to nontraditional jobs. In 2007—by a 5-4 vote, with Justice Alito writing the Court's opinion—the Court restricted the ability of Lilly Ledbetter, one of the few female managers at a manufacturing plant, to bring suit challenging that she was paid significantly less than her male counterparts.

In spite of these important turnarounds, the main effect of *Bush v. Gore* isn't so much the substitution of Chief Justice Roberts and Justice Alito for Chief Justice Rehnquist and Justice O'Connor. Rather, it's the possible loss of two opportunities for would-have-been President Al Gore to select their successors. On a Court with two more Democratic-nominated justices, the generally conservative Justice Kennedy would likely not be the swing vote as he is today. Instead those two more moderate—or even liberal—

justices might form a voting majority along with Justices Sotomayor, Ginsburg, Breyer, and Kagan. That Court might be more committed to equality, to individual litigants' access to the justice system, and to a host of other constitutional claims than has been the Court that *Bush v. Gore* produced.

7. The Wages of Watergate

It has now been more than 40 years since the Watergate break-in, which precipitated modern efforts to respond to the dangers of unfettered political spending. Yet our political system is now more awash than ever in secret money. Why? Much of the answer lies in the interaction between Supreme Court decisions and post-Watergate reforms.

In the wake of the scandal, the 1974 amendments to the Federal Election Campaign Act (FECA) sought to limit both political contributions and expenditures. But in its foundational decision in *Buckley v. Valeo* (1976), a challenge to the FECA amendments, the Supreme Court drew a sharp distinction between these two forms of political spending. It upheld stringent limits on contributions to other people's campaigns, on the theory that these limits mark a reasonable response to the potential for quid pro quo corruption or the appearance of corruption. But the Court refused to limit political expenditures, on the theory that "the First Amendment denies government the power to determine that spending to promote one's political views is wasteful, excessive, or unwise."

In drawing this distinction, the Court created a statute that no sensible legislature would have passed. *Buckley* accelerated two existing unhealthy trends in American politics.

First, it gave a decided advantage to rich candidates: they could spend unlimited amounts of their own money while their opponents had to raise it in relatively small increments. The Roberts Court exacerbated this problem with its 2011 decision in *Arizona Free Enterprise Club's Freedom Club PAC v. Bennett* (a case whose name sounds like nothing so much as a winner at the Westminster Kennel Club's dog show). There, the Court held that the First

Amendment bars states from providing additional funds to equalize the playing field for candidates who agree to forgo private contributions and accept public financing.

Second, because *Buckley* protected candidates' right to spend however much they can raise while limiting how they can raise it, the decision forced candidates to devote ever-increasing attention to fundraising at the expense of other activities, such as doing their jobs. By 2012, when the average winning campaign for a House seat cost roughly $1.5 million, members of Congress had to raise about $85 every hour of every day during their two-year terms. The framers' idea that frequent elections would make the House responsive to the people was turned on its head: frequent elections now render members of the House particularly dependent on special interest groups that can help them raise large amounts of money.

A third effect of *Buckley* was harder to envision at the time of the Court's decision, and has proven even more pernicious. Even as the Court was upholding FECA's disclosure rules—which require candidates for federal office to identify all individuals who contribute more than $200 in an election cycle—its decision was driving money into new, and less accountable, channels.

Prior to Watergate, political spending typically took the form of contributions to candidates or political parties. The corrosive effects of that money were at least tempered by strong incentives for candidates and parties to build coalitions and to focus on a range of issues. And voters had the opportunity to hold those candidates accountable for the way they raised and spent that money.

After *Buckley*, money flowed away from candidates and political parties and toward political action committees (PACs). PACs originated in a 1940s effort by unions to coordinate individual contributions from their members, and their number and influence exploded thanks to *Buckley*. PACs present a serious challenge to the health of the political system because, in contrast to parties, they frequently focus on only a single issue. They can form and dissolve within individual election cycles. They often have names that obscure more than they reveal, so that it is difficult for voters to intelligently assess the signals that PAC spending sends.

The *Buckley* framework transformed PACs. The original PACs were designed to funnel money to candidates. But because contributions by PACs to candidates, like contributions by individuals, could be strictly limited, PACs turned to making "independent expenditures," which, in *Buckley*, the Supreme Court had refused to limit because it saw no risk of corruption. "Independent," however, is a somewhat elastic term. Candidates know which PACs support them. And while it is theoretically possible that a PAC's work on a candidate's behalf will be so counterproductive that he won't appreciate it, that is rarely the case.

The Court itself sometimes confuses the categories of contributions and expenditures and, in so doing, has shown that the distinction it drew is not nearly as clean as it may think. In *Caperton v. A.T. Massey Coal Co.* (2009), Justice Kennedy's opinion for the Court held that an elected state court judge violated due process by sitting on a case involving a corporate executive who had made "extraordinary" and exceptionally large "campaign contributions" to the judge. In fact the executive had contributed only a thousand dollars (the statutory maximum) to the judge's campaign. That hardly seems extraordinary. The problem more likely was his $500,000 independent expenditure supporting the campaign and his roughly $2.5 million donation to the "And For The Sake of the Kids" PAC, which went after the judge's opponent.

Over the years campaign finance law has become a three-way dance involving the Court, reformers, and political spenders. The Court's increasingly robust First Amendment doctrine—holding, for example, that corporations enjoy the same right to engage in political speech as individuals—has hemmed in reform efforts. *Citizens United v. Federal Election Commission* (2010) categorically rejected regulation on the basis of money's corrosive effect on politics and freed corporations and unions to use general treasury funds for independent expenditures. *Arizona Free Enterprise Club* made it far less feasible to create workable public financing regimes.

At the same time, sophisticated political actors have responded to every reform by devising new methods for shoveling money into the system. The super PAC is one recent example. Super PACs, unlike earlier PACs, can raise unlimited funds from individuals and corporations. And because the law permits them to report their donors on a quarterly basis, it is possible to shield funders' identities until an election is over.

Perhaps even more troubling is the apparent movement of large amounts of political money into 501(c) groups, so named because they are organized under section 501(c) of the Internal Revenue Code. These groups are not required to identify their donors at all. According to the Center for Responsive Politics, outside interest groups are now outspending the political parties—by more than $100 million over the past two years—and the portion of that spending attributable to 501(c) groups has risen from 1 percent in 2006 to nearly half today. Most strikingly, the Center concludes, "Seventy-two percent of political advertising spending by outside groups in 2010 came from sources that were prohibited from spending money in 2006."

The effect on our politics is not just that well-heeled interests enjoy a tremendous advantage, although that is bad enough in itself. The corrosion is also seen in the nature of our political discourse. Shadow groups seem particularly prone to generating polarizing and negative sound bites rather than discussing the real issues facing the electorate.

However, money is only one symptom of a deeper political pathology. We hear a flood of stories and arguments about campaign finance, but relatively little serious popular attention is paid to gerrymandering, restrictive registration requirements, and electoral administration. Even less concern is given to the absence of any real civics education in this era of high-stakes testing and underfunded public schools. As Sam Issacharoff and I observed a more than a dozen years ago in an article on the hydraulics of campaign finance reform:

> The First Amendment and political spending are only two of the many institutional structures within which our politics take place. These structures, which we often take for granted, powerfully shape our sense of the politically possible and what the baseline for a purer politics should be.

Until concerned citizens address these deep structural problems, we are unlikely to persuade either the wider American public to adopt effective campaign finance regulations or the Supreme Court to uphold them.

8. Me, Inc.

When the Supreme Court heard *Santa Clara County v. Southern Pacific Railroad Co.* in 1886, few would have pegged the case as a turning point in constitutional law. The matter at hand seemed highly technical: could California increase the property tax owed by a railroad if the railroad built fences on its property?

As it turned out, the Court ruled unanimously in the railroad's favor. And in so doing, the Court casually affirmed the railroad's argument that corporations are "persons" within the meaning of the Fourteenth Amendment, which provides that no state shall "deprive any person of life, liberty, or property, without due process of law; nor deny to any person within its jurisdiction the equal protection of the laws." So certain were the justices of the Fourteenth Amendment's applicability that their opinion did not engage the issue, but the Court reporter recorded the justices' perspective on the topic:

> Before argument Mr. Chief Justice Waite said: 'The Court does not wish to hear argument on the question whether the provision in the Fourteenth Amendment to the Constitution which forbids a state to deny to any person within its jurisdiction the equal protection of the laws applies to these corporations. We are all of opinion that it does.'

That statement marks the origin of the view that corporations are persons as a matter of constitutional law. This played a central role in the 2010 decision in *Citizens United v. Federal Election Commission*, which struck down portions of the Bipartisan Campaign Reform Act that restricted corporate spending on electioneering communications in the run-up to a federal election. The Court declared that

Congress could not discriminate between election-eering communications according to the identity of the speaker: since individual human beings clearly have a First Amendment right to speak about candidates during the election process, so too must corporations.

Much criticism of the *Citizens United* decision has focused on whether corporations should have rights under the Constitution. This critique is mistaken. Corporations come in many forms, ranging from large, publicly traded profit-driven companies (think IBM) to smaller, ideologically motivated nonprofits (the American Civil Liberties Union or the Audubon Society) with many others in between (your local newspaper). The diverse nature of corporations may mean that some corporations have stronger claims than others with respect to particular rights, but on the whole it is clear that our democracy could not function if corporations received no constitutional protection. One of the most famous First Amendment decisions of the Warren Court, *New York Times v. Sullivan* (1964), protected a for-profit newspaper from a libel suit for publishing a paid advertisement criticizing a public official. Many foundational freedom-of-association cases likewise involve corporations, such as the NAACP. And even with respect to purely economic rights, it is hard to argue persuasively that the government should have no obligation to provide due process to corporations before imposing fines or condemning their property.

So corporations are entitled to constitutional protection. But are they entitled to the same protection as living, breathing human beings? In *Federal Communications Commission v. AT&T* (2011), the Supreme Court suggested they are not. The Court refused to extend to AT&T a provision of the Freedom of Information Act that exempts the disclosure of material that might cause "an unwarranted invasion of personal privacy." A corporation, Chief Justice Roberts said, does not have the "type of privacy evocative of human concerns." Similarly, corporations cannot invoke the Fifth Amendment's protection against self-incrimination.

Even if the Court decided that corporations are in every way like persons, there might be limits on the corporate role in politics. When faced with the issue of popular confidence in the democratic process, courts have agreed that the speech rights of flesh-and-blood persons may be bounded. The Hatch Act, for example, forbids government employees from engaging in partisan political activity, including some activities in their off time.

In fact, when it comes to a willingness to restrict constitutional rights in the name of confidence in the democratic process, the Court's decisions show a troubling and puzzling asymmetry in favor of corporations. A few years ago, the Court upheld Indiana's draconian voter-identification statute, which threatened to deny the fundamental right to vote to thousands of individuals who lack government-issued photo ID. The Court asserted, "Public confidence in the integrity of the electoral process has independent significance, because it encourages citizen participation in the democratic process." The Court nowhere explains why a similar rationale should not apply to political spending. Several legislatures think it should and have concluded that citizens are less likely to participate in a process they think is rigged in favor of large corporate interests.

The real issue, then, is not whether corporations deserve some constitutional protections: they do. The issue is whether there is something about the nature of corporations that makes it appropriate to limit their involvement in the political process. The Court has foreclosed the most common affirmative answer to that question: corporations have accumulated enormous wealth, which enables them to distort a political process that rests on a commitment to equality, embodied most prominently in the principle of one person, one vote. The *Citizens United* decision rejected this argument by overruling a prior holding in *Austin v. Michigan Chamber of Commerce* (1990).

In *Austin* the Court decided that the government has a compelling interest in preventing "the corrosive and distorting effects of immense aggregations of wealth that are accumulated with the help of the corporate form and that have little or no correlation to the public's support for the corporation's political ideas." But in *Citizens United*, the Court went the other way, declaring that refusing to limit political speech "based on a speaker's wealth is a necessary consequence of the premise that the First Amendment generally prohibits the suppression of political speech based on the speaker's identity." Given the vehemence with which five justices embraced this position, there is little prospect of reviving the logic of *Austin* in the foreseeable future.

The rejoinder that corporate wealth is often amassed from people who don't share a company's political views—people might eat at Chick-fil-A because they like the food and not because they share the owners' conservative perspective—is no less true of individuals: even people who disagree with Bill

Gates's politics use Windows, and this shouldn't prevent him exercising his right to political speech using the wealth he has accumulated.

The better argument in favor of limiting partisan political spending by large, publicly traded corporations rests, ironically, on the fact that corporations are made up of people. Under current law the actual owners of corporations—their shareholders—have little say in how corporations make decisions in the political arena. That corporate managers might spend corporate funds not to maximize the shareholders' welfare but to maximize their own is a very real danger. Many shares are owned by mutual funds and pension funds that in turn are owned by individual citizens who often have political convictions that matter to them more than maximizing the profitability of the corporations whose stock forms part of their retirement savings. Indeed, those political commitments may be sharply at odds with the economic interests of the corporate managers who are making decisions about corporate political spending. The law should not force citizens to forgo beneficial investments in order to avoid subsidizing their political opponents.

All of which is to say that campaign finance regulation is tricky. As critics of regulation—including Justices Scalia and Kennedy—observe, there are real risks that incumbents will pass regulations that protect themselves from electoral challenge. And, as I explained in the previous chapter, federal campaign finance legislation often results only in shifting sources of money and influence—from individuals to PACs to 527s. But one thing is clear: the observation that corporations have rights should not end the debate about the constitutionality of regulation.

9. Votes Behind Bars

Nearly half a century ago, Isaiah Berlin delivered an extraordinarily influential lecture called "Two Concepts of Liberty." The negative concept consists in freedom *from*—"warding off interference" from external forces. By contrast, the positive concept consists in freedom *to*—to be "a doer—deciding, not being decided for." Democracy requires both forms, but current constitutional doctrine adopts an unduly negative approach.

This is especially the case when it comes to political voice. The Supreme Court has resisted attempts to constrain the political impact of money, most notoriously in *Citizens United v. Federal Election Commission* (2010). But just as telling is *Arizona Free Enterprise*

Club's Freedom Club PAC v. Bennett (2011), where the Court hobbled the states' ability to construct public financing systems. Adjusting the funds available to candidates who accept public financing somehow burdens privately financed candidates' freedom, according to the justices.

The Court's rationale in campaign finance cases calls on protection of free speech, which invokes a negative concept of liberty because the freedom of speech guaranteed by the First Amendment is largely exercised without government assistance. (As A.J. Liebling memorably observed with respect to another branch of the First Amendment, freedom of the press is reserved only for those who own one.) Political speech, the Court points out, is "an essential mechanism of democracy, for it is the means to hold officials accountable to the people." True enough.

Yet voting is surely an equally essential mechanism of democracy, and arguably a more direct means of holding officials accountable, but the Court has upheld laws that burden casting a ballot, a positive liberty. In *Crawford v. Marion County Election Board* (2008), the Court rejected a challenge to an Indiana law requiring already-registered voters to present government-issued photo identification at the polls. (Disclosure: I helped to represent the plaintiffs in the case.) The justices in the majority did not agree on every element of the case, but, after recognizing that Indiana could not point to a single example, ever, of impersonation that would have been prevented by an ID requirement, the Court accepted Indiana's argument that ID prevents fraud and enhances "public confidence" in the election process. By contrast, the Court has essentially rejected this rationale in the political-spending context.

The Court's strikingly different treatment of burdens on political spending and on voting reflects this positive-negative divide. Effective exercise of the right to vote depends on affirmative government support. A citizen who is handed an official ballot written in a language she does not understand may effectively be denied the right to vote. If the government uses unreliable voting machines or staffs polling places with badly trained workers, citizens may effectively be prevented from voting by the press of other responsibilities that preclude waiting in line for hours. Voter ID laws disenfranchise individuals who find it difficult or impossible to obtain government-issued documents.

A superficial reading of the Constitution might support the Court's opinions. Although the Constitution is filled with provisions mentioning the "right to vote," the most explicit protections are phrased almost entirely in negative terms: they prohibit particular forms of disenfranchisement. The Fifteenth and Nineteenth Amendments, for example, forbid denial of the right to vote "on account of race" or "sex"; the Twenty-Fourth, "by reason of failure to pay any poll tax."

In light of this language, in 1875 the Supreme Court declared itself "unanimously of the opinion that the Constitution of the United States does not confer the right of suffrage upon any one." To be sure, the equal protection clause provides one important qualification: the government cannot arbitrarily treat voters unequally. During the 2012 election, a federal court of appeals relied on the clause to hold that if Ohio permitted military voters to cast early ballots the weekend before the November election, it had to make early voting available to other voters on the same terms. But the court was careful to acknowledge that Ohio had not been constitutionally required to offer early voting at all.

The consequences of adopting an essentially negative approach to political voice extend beyond enhanced protection for the political deployment of concentrated wealth and beyond new rules, such as voter ID requirements, that block full participation. The negative approach underwrites a practice that continues to set the United States apart among advanced democracies: disenfranchising millions of citizens due to criminal convictions. Even incarcerated prisoners vote in countries as otherwise diverse as the Czech Republic, Denmark, France, Israel, Japan,

Kenya, the Netherlands, and Zimbabwe. In the last dozen years, the highest courts of Canada and South Africa and the European Court of Human Rights have each issued opinions recognizing the voting rights of incarcerated citizens.

As of 2010 more than 5.85 million American citizens were disenfranchised as a result of criminal convictions. Only a quarter of those individuals were then incarcerated. Roughly 30 percent were on probation or parole. The remaining 45 percent were ex-offenders, many disenfranchised for life as a result of felony convictions involving small amounts of drugs or nonviolent crimes that never resulted in prison sentences.

Such extensive disenfranchisement would be distressing in any event, but it becomes even more troubling in light of the dramatic effect it has on the black community. More than 2 million African Americans currently are stripped of their right to vote. That's more than the number of African Americans who gained the franchise in 1870 thanks to the

Fifteenth Amendment. Precedent permits offender disenfranchisement unless challengers can show that states adopted or have maintained their practice for purposefully discriminatory reasons, a nearly insurmountable hurdle. In 2005, for example, the Supreme Court refused to review Florida's lifetime offender disenfranchisement provision even though the ban had been adopted in 1868 precisely for the purpose of disenfranchising newly freed slaves. Lower federal courts acknowledged this unconstitutional motivation but held that the taint somehow had dissipated by 1968, when Florida renewed the ban without giving any reasons for doing so.

Offender disenfranchisement statutes impair the voting rights of people beyond the offenders themselves. Flawed records and negligent purges result in thousands of eligible voters being excluded. More than 2,400 black voters in Florida were erroneously purged before the 2000 election, dwarfing George W. Bush's 537-vote margin of victory. And punitive offender disenfranchisement statutes deprive the black community as a whole of political power, which in turn skews election results to the right and creates legislative bodies hostile to civil rights and economic justice for the franchised and disenfranchised alike.

Faced with these problems, some activists and scholars suggest the need for a new constitutional amendment recognizing the affirmative right to vote. I think a better approach lies in reviving the late legal scholar Charles Black's approach to constitutional reasoning. Black argued that the overall structure of the Constitution presupposes free and fair elections in which all qualified citizens can participate. Individual amendments expanding the electorate reflect this general principle. Abolishing poll taxes, for instance, stands for a fundamental commitment to eliminating barriers to registration and to ensuring that wealth is not the means of accessing politics.

And the Court should apply to offender disenfranchisement statutes a principle it has already recognized elsewhere: whether a punishment violates the Eighth Amendment's bar on cruel and unusual punishment "is judged not by the standards that prevailed in 1685 . . . or when the Bill of Rights was adopted," but instead by "the evolving standards of decency that mark the progress of a maturing society."

Today, continuing to disenfranchise millions of our fellow citizens cannot survive that test of evolving standards. Public opinion surveys show strong support for reinstating the voting rights of offenders who have completed their sentences or who are on probation or parole. In recent years several states have liberalized their offender disenfranchisement statutes without waiting for the Supreme Court to act. Their actions should remind us that constitutional values may sometimes be realized more fully through the political process than through constitutional litigation.

Part III

*Reasoning Together
About Our Rights*

10. Gideon's Muted Trumpet

LAST SPRING MARKED THE 50TH ANNIVERSARY of *Gideon v. Wainwright*, in which the Supreme Court considered the Sixth Amendment's guarantee that "in all criminal prosecutions, the accused shall enjoy the right . . . to have the Assistance of Counsel for his defence." The Court unanimously interpreted the Amendment as requiring that states provide attorneys for defendants who lack the resources to hire them privately. The "noble ideal" that "every defendant stands equal before the law," Justice Hugo Black's opinion declared, "cannot be realized if the poor man charged with crime has to face his accusers without a lawyer to assist him." Given an attorney for his retrial, Clarence Gideon was acquitted.

Today, the vast majority of criminal defendants depend on appointed counsel to represent them, and the quality of representation varies wildly.

At one end of the spectrum, indigent defendants represented by some public defender organizations receive counsel every bit as expert as the most well-heeled client could buy. But the majority of the states that operate public defender services fail to meet the federal government's standards for attorneys' maximum caseloads. And many defendants receive dreadful representation: a shockingly high percentage of defendants sentenced to death were represented by lawyers who were either disciplined or disbarred at some point in their careers, often within a few years of the defendants' trials. Indeed, there are enough instances of lawyers who literally slept through their clients' trials to produce a grotesque jurisprudence regarding when somnolence rises—or sinks—to the level of a Sixth Amendment violation.

The Supreme Court has recognized that just any counsel isn't good enough. But the Court's standard for constitutionally ineffective assistance, announced in *Strickland v. Washington* (1984), makes it extremely hard for a defendant to argue that his lawyer failed him. A defendant challenging his conviction not only has to show that his lawyer's performance fell below a relatively deferential bar, but also has to prove prejudice—that is, a reasonable probability that, but for the errors, the outcome would have been different. By contrast, for most other constitutional violations, the burden is on the government to show the error was harmless. And although in recent years the Court has been somewhat more vigilant in enforcing the Sixth Amendment—requiring in *Padilla v. Kentucky* (2010), for instance, that lawyers provide accurate information to noncitizen clients about the immigration consequences of pleading guilty—its promise all too often goes unfulfilled.

Consider two powerful illustrations of how *Gideon*'s trumpet—to borrow from the title of the late Anthony Lewis's superb 1964 book about the case—has been muted.

One is *Boyer v. Louisiana.* Boyer, who has a borderline I.Q., a third-grade reading level, and a history of mental illness, had admitted under police interrogation to killing the victim, but his statement did not match the physical evidence in several relevant respects. There was also at least one other plausible suspect. Nonetheless, the state charged him with capital murder in 2002.

Louisiana has a long history of underfunding its indigent defense system, and at the time Boyer was charged, the state provided no resources to indigent defense. Local indigent defender boards were funded essentially by revenue from traffic tickets, which fluctuated dramatically from year to year.

In Boyer's case, the public defender was unavailable due to a conflict of interest. So the judge drafted a practitioner from a small firm to represent Boyer. But there were no funds available to compensate the lawyer for the hundreds of hours he would be required to devote to the case or for out-of-pocket litigation expenses. The next five years were consumed by proceedings trying to obtain those funds. Those proceedings were repeatedly postponed to await decisions in parallel cases also involving unfunded indigent defense.

When Boyer's attorney moved to dismiss the charges against his client for violation of a different provision of the Sixth Amendment—the right to a speedy trial—he was forced to abandon that claim because, in a Kafkaesque twist, the very lack of funds that had caused the delay had also prevented him from showing why the delay had impaired his ability to mount an effective defense.

In the end, the state abandoned the capital charge against Boyer so that it could proceed against him on a lesser charge for which he could be represented by a less experienced attorney. By the time of the trial, in 2009, a number of potentially relevant witnesses had either died or gone missing. Boyer was convicted by a non-unanimous jury (a practice permitted only in Louisiana and Oregon) and sentenced to life in prison without the possibility of parole.

On appeal, the state appellate court recognized that the extraordinary delay in bringing Boyer to trial raised a red flag under the Supreme Court's foundational speedy trial case, *Barker v. Wingo* (1972). But in another twist, it held that the "funding crisis" was a "cause beyond the control of the state," and therefore the prosecution had proceeded properly.

While the Supreme Court originally agreed to hear Boyer's claim that he had been deprived of his right to a speedy trial, it later dismissed his petition as "improvidently granted." Thus the Court avoided confronting the question of whether Louisiana's entire system is constitutionally deficient.

Another example of the Sixth Amendment's false promise arises from more mundane sources than Boyer's murder charge: misdemeanor cases. A decade after *Gideon*, in *Argersinger v. Hamlin* (1972), the Court extended *Gideon*, which applied only to felony cases, to all criminal prosecutions, including misdemeanors, in which jail time is imposed. The government can prosecute misdemeanors without providing counsel to indigent defendants, but unless the defendant waives his right to counsel, the judge cannot order the defendant to serve time if he is convicted.

And yet, as a practical matter, misdemeanor defendants may face a cruel dilemma. A 2009 investigative series in the *San Jose Mercury News* discovered that in Santa Clara County, California, defendants charged with misdemeanors were not provided attorneys at arraignment, generally their first court appearance. Instead, they faced the option of asking for a lawyer—in which case they might be kept in custody until one is appointed—or of pleading guilty on the spot. Without a lawyer at arraignment, many defendants will find it difficult to get pretrial release, as the legal scholar Douglas Colbert has shown.

The upshot is that unrepresented defendants often end up getting the equivalent of a jail sentence, only they serve it *before* they've been convicted.

And in many cases, they might never be convicted if they receive competent counsel. A *Mercury*

News study of roughly 250 defendants charged with resisting arrest found that while almost half of the represented defendants had their charges reduced or dropped altogether, only one in ten self-represented defendants did. Moreover, defendants who plead guilty simply to avoid being locked up while they wait for a lawyer to be appointed will be stuck with criminal records and all the consequences they entail.

Underfunding misdemeanor defense creates its own problems. In Detroit, according to a 2008 National Legal Aid & Defender Association report, lawyers spend around half an hour, on average, on each misdemeanor case.

Misdemeanor cases may not be as striking as Jonathan Boyer's, but they too demonstrate the significant costs inflicted by the failure to honor *Gideon*. As Justice Black put it 50 years ago, "Lawyers in criminal courts are necessities, not luxuries."

11. The Cost of Death

Samuel Johnson famously remarked, "When a man knows he is to be hanged in a fortnight, it concentrates his mind wonderfully." But precisely because it so concentrates the public mind, capital punishment has distorted the criminal justice system. Over the past 40 years, while the Supreme Court has been "tinker[ing] with the machinery of death," in Justice Harry Blackmun's haunting phrase, other components of the system have broken down untended.

In 1972, by a vote of 5-4, the Supreme Court struck down all capital punishment statutes in the United States. While three justices were prepared to hold the death penalty unconstitutional under all circumstances, two others focused on the fact that existing statutes led to arbitrary decisions that followed no legal standards. As Justice Potter Stewart put it, capital punishment violated the cruel and unusual punishment clause of the Eighth Amendment because being sentenced to death was like "being struck by lightning."

Many states responded by enacting new capital punishment statutes that purported to formalize decision-making. In 1976 the Supreme Court upheld several of these efforts, pointing to key procedural safeguards, such as the creation of a separate penalty phase to determine whether the defendant deserves to die. In this penalty phase, defense counsel can present a broad range of mitigating evidence that may diminish the defendant's culpability or incline a judge or jury to mercy.

But too often the formal safeguards that reassured the Court have proved illusory in practice. Underfunded, untrained, or outright incompetent lawyers often fail to provide their clients even minimally adequate representation. A 1990 study by the *National Law Journal* found that a quarter of the inmates then on Kentucky's death row had been represented at their trials by lawyers who were later disbarred, suspended from practice, or convicted of crimes. A capital defendant in Georgia was assigned a lawyer who knew the name of only a single criminal law opinion decided by any court.

And however unwilling the Supreme Court has been to ensure that capital defendants receive truly competent representation—its interpretation of the Sixth Amendment's guarantee of effective assistance of counsel sets the bar so low that courts have upheld convictions in cases where the lawyer was actually asleep during part of the proceedings—it has been even less willing to police systemic unfairness in who is targeted for the most awesome punishment. In *McClesky v. Kemp* (1987) the Court rejected powerful statistical evidence showing that the death penalty in Georgia was infected by racial disparities: black defendants convicted of killing white victims were far more likely to be sentenced to death than any other group. Justice Lewis Powell's opinion was unusually candid in explaining why the Court could not accept McClesky's claim: "Taken to its logical conclusion," Justice Powell wrote, McClesky's position "throws into serious question the principles that underlie our entire criminal justice system." Racial disparities marbled the criminal justice system, so they had to be ignored.

Because the Court and Congress convinced themselves that death row inmates were dragging out the process of post-conviction appeals, they have dramatically restricted the ability of all defendants to seek habeas corpus, the primary vehicle for bringing constitutional challenges against state court convictions. The provisions of the Antiterrorism and Effective Death Penalty Act of 1996 (AEDPA) create a procedural obstacle course that prevents federal courts from addressing the merits of a defendant's constitutional claims.

For example, in its 2011 term, the Court confronted the case of Cory Maples, a death row inmate in Alabama who had been unable to get the federal courts to hear his claim that his trial lawyer was ineffective at his sentencing. The reason? The volunteer lawyers who later represented him moved on to new jobs, and when the state court ruled against his claim, there was no one at their former law firm to receive the letter announcing the decision. The letter was stamped "Return to Sender," and the deadline for appeal passed before anyone noticed. As a result, lower federal courts accepted the state's argument that Maples had "defaulted" his claims. Justice Ginsburg's opinion for the Court in *Maples v. Thomas* held that because Maples's attorneys had completely abandoned him, he had shown an external "cause" for his failure to pursue his claims in a timely manner. But she refused to "disturb" the general rule that "negligence on the part of a prisoner's postconviction attorney does not qualify as 'cause,'" and thus a prisoner is out of luck when his lawyer fails him. Only because Maples had suffered, in Justice Alito's words, "a veritable perfect storm of misfortune" did the Supreme

Court intervene. A defendant who had simply had incompetent habeas representation, rather than no representation at all, would have been out of luck.

The same term, the Supreme Court (over the dissent of Justices Sotomayor and Kagan) denied a petition for certiorari filed by Duane Buck, whose death sentence Texas sought to insulate from federal review despite the fact that, under questioning from a prosecutor, a psychologist told the jury that being black "increases [Buck's] future dangerousness"—a necessary element for a death sentence under that state's law. As of spring 2013, despite a vigorous effort by bar organizations, civil rights groups, and a broad range of Texas public officials, Buck remains on death row while another round of appeals works its way through the Texas court system.

Cases such as these—not to mention the recent execution of Troy Davis, which spurred worldwide protests—receive focused attention both inside and outside the Court. The Court's rules single out capital cases for special treatment, directing that the notation "CAPITAL CASE" appear at the beginning of any such request for review and mandating that the government, which often waives its right to reply, file a response. The clerk's office has a special staff attorney charged with overseeing the voluminous, often last-minute filings in death penalty cases. The justices and their law clerks often scrutinize the filings with great care. The bar has also responded: death row inmates typically receive superb legal assistance before the Supreme Court. Former Bush Administration Solicitor General Gregory Garre represented Maples. Current Solicitor General Donald Verrilli previously represented several death row inmates pro bono before the Court.

But the concentration on capital cases comes at a cost. Ineffective trial lawyers, inconclusive evidence, inconsistent testimony, and impenetrable procedural thickets are hardly unique to capital cases. Nonetheless, the Court is far less likely to pay attention to these claims when the consequences to the defendant seem less harsh. Criminal law and procedure scholars such as Robert Weisberg of Stanford and Douglas Berman of Ohio State have described how the Court's concern with death leads it to shortchange the constitutional claims of defendants facing lesser punishments. Berman has calculated that about one in ten thousand state felony sentences is a death sentence, yet the Court devotes more resources to reviewing death sentences than to reviewing claims in all other criminal cases combined. And while the Court has repeatedly considered whether a death sentence is proportionate to a particular class of crimes—for example, barring death sentences for individuals not convicted of homicide or for juvenile or mentally retarded defendants—it has set virtually no limits on the severity of prison sentences. In the 40 years that the Court has been actively policing capital punishment, prison sentences have lengthened and the U.S. prison population has skyrocketed. With execution at the top end of the scale of punishment, a life sentence begins to look something like leniency, and other sentences are inflated in turn.

Capital cases also consume thousands of hours of legal services from some of the finest legal minds in America. The time those lawyers spend challenging death sentences of inmates whose guilt is not seriously in doubt could be spent preventing and remedying wrongful convictions, ensuring that all defendants receive prompt appointment of competent counsel, and attacking draconian prison conditions, not to mention providing civil justice to poor and disenfranchised people. But as long as the death penalty is with us, superb and committed lawyers at organizations such as the Southern Center for Human Rights, the Equal Justice Initiative, and the NAACP Legal Defense and Educational Fund will find themselves defending the lives of a few while the lives of many others continue to be ruined by pervasive flaws in our criminal justice system.

12. What's a Right Without a Remedy?

IN THE MOMENTOUS 1803 CASE *MARBURY V. Madison*, Chief Justice John Marshall observed that the "very essence of civil liberty certainly consists in the right of every individual to claim the protection of the laws, whenever he receives an injury" and warned that a government cannot be called a "government of laws, and not of men . . . . if the laws furnish no remedy for the violation of a vested legal right."

When the government itself violates individuals' rights, it is especially important for courts to furnish a remedy. To be sure, providing remedies to the victims of unconstitutional conduct after the fact is often at best an imperfect solution. While money plausibly provides full compensation to, say, a government worker denied income while suspended for engaging in First Amendment–protected activity, it may be far less effective in a case involving an unconstitutional strip search: Can money really restore the sense of security that the victim has lost? If not, perhaps it can at least enable her to begin rebuilding her life.

Ideally, backward-looking remedies can deter future violations. If government officials or agencies know that they will be held to account, they will be less likely to commit violations in the first place. And injunctive remedies—judicial orders either to stop engaging in a particular practice (for example, racial profiling of motorists) or to start doing something the government has so far failed to do (for example, issuing marriage licenses to same-sex couples)—have been critical to enforcing civil rights and civil liberties.

More broadly, judicial remedies perform an important expressive function: they drive home to the public that the law takes constitutional violations seriously. This can galvanize popular movements to vindicate constitutional values even more fully. For example, the Supreme Court's decisions in *Brown v. Board of Education* (1954–55), held that purposeful racial segregation of public schools violated the Fourteenth Amendment's equal protection clause and ordered that school boards dismantle their dual school systems. The *Brown* decisions by themselves achieved very little actual integration, but the Court's condemnation of segregation provided critical support to a mass movement that culminated in statutes such as the Civil Rights Act of 1964, which crafted more effective tools for dismantling Jim Crow in schools, public accommodation, employment, and housing.

So a lot depends on the availability of a remedy: when the courts refuse to provide one, rights can be reduced to mere lines on paper.

Indeed, recent years have shown a troubling trend as the Supreme Court has retrenched on protecting civil rights and civil liberties in two important ways. Sometimes the Court has straightforwardly redefined an underlying right in more limited terms. For example, in *Montejo v. Louisiana* (2009) the Court narrowed Sixth Amendment protections against police interrogation of criminal defendants without their lawyers being present. And in *Gonzales v. Carhart* (2007) the Court upheld restrictions on abortion rights almost identical to those it had earlier struck down. (I represented the California Medical Association as an amicus curiae in the case.)

The second approach is more insidious. Here the Court leaves the formal right in place but constricts the remedial machinery. At best, this will dilute the value of the right, since some violations will go unremedied. At worst, it may signal potential wrongdoers that they can infringe the right with impunity.

Remedial abridgment is a pervasive tool of the contemporary Supreme Court. One area in which it often is used is criminal procedure. For example, for decades the so-called exclusionary rule forbade prosecutors from using evidence obtained through unconstitutional searches or impermissible interrogation techniques. But while the Burger, Rehnquist, and Roberts Courts have left in place most of the Warren Court's restrictions on police activity, they have developed a series of what criminal procedure scholar Carol Steiker calls "inclusionary" rules: exceptions to the exclusionary rule that result in many defendants being convicted on the basis of illegally obtained evidence. These inclusionary rules weaken the deterrent force of the exclusionary rule by signaling to police that illegally obtained evidence won't be worthless.

In its cases cutting back on the exclusionary rule, the Court often points to the availability of alternative mechanisms for enforcing the Fourth Amendment's prohibition of unconstitutional searches and seizures. The Court has repeatedly highlighted the option to seek civil damages under a Reconstruction-era statute (42 U.S.C. § 1983), which authorizes suits against state and local officials and governments that deprive individuals of their constitutional rights. Yet the Court has substantially weakened the section 1983 remedy at precisely the time that it has weakened the exclusionary rule, engaging in a sort of shell game in which the presence of each remedy serves to justify weakening the protections of the other.

For example, section 1983 suits are subject to an increasingly government-friendly doctrine of "qualified immunity," which shields officials from liability unless they violate constitutional rules that were "clearly established" at the time of the offense. To get a sense of how protective that rule is, consider *Wilson v. Layne* (1999). First the Supreme Court held unanimously that, according to the Fourth Amendment's prohibition of unreasonable searches, law enforcement officials could not bring the media uninvited into people's homes (think *Cops*). Then the Court held, 8-1, that until it issued its unanimous opinion, it would not have been clear that such intrusions were impermissible.

Although qualified immunity provides no barrier to suits against governments themselves, the Court has developed other doctrines to shield them. A particularly callous example of the Court's willingness to leave victims of even atrocious constitutional violations uncompensated came in *Connick v. Thompson* (2011). There, the Court tossed out the $14 million jury verdict John Thompson obtained against the Orleans Parish District Attorney's Office after he spent fourteen years in solitary confinement on death row for a murder he did not commit. Prosecutors had deliberately withheld favorable evidence from his lawyers. The Court did not contest that the prosecutors' behavior violated clear constitutional standards. But it held that the government could not be held liable because it was not sufficiently obvious that the failure to train its prosecutors about their constitutional responsibilities would cause such violations. (I represented a group of former high-level officials in the Department of Justice, from Republican and Democratic administrations alike, who filed an amicus brief stressing the necessity of such training.)

The trend continued in *Minneci v. Pollard* (2012). In that case the Court ruled that federal prisoners held in private facilities (as opposed to ones run by the Bureau of Prisons) cannot seek damages in federal court for violations of the Eighth Amendment's prohibition of cruel and unusual punishment. Sure, the Eighth Amendment *applies*: privately run prisons, like government-run ones, cannot deny inmates adequate medical care or nutrition, or physically mistreat them. But when they do, the inmates' only resort is to go into state court under a state-law theory, such as medical malpractice. They cannot vindicate their constitutional claims directly.

Decisions such as *Connick v. Thompson* or the recent series of cases ejecting workers and consumers from the courts and forcing them into arbitration—often preventing victims banding together as a class—don't explicitly change what the law tells governments or businesses they can or cannot do. But these decisions can have that effect, by making it harder for victims of wrongful conduct to exercise their rights. They thus betray the Supreme Court's long-ago promise that it would ensure a government of laws.

13. When the Umpire Throws the Pitches

DURING HIS CONFIRMATION HEARINGS, CHIEF Justice Roberts famously compared judges to umpires. The analogy was designed to convey an image of judicial modesty: judges, like umpires, play a "limited role," impartially applying rules made by others rather than serving as partisans for one team or another. And he assured the Senate that he would "remember that it's my job to call balls and strikes and not to pitch or bat."

Umpires leave the tactical choices to the teams. As we saw in Chapter 4, that kind of reserve led Alexander Hamilton, in *Federalist* No. 78, to describe the judiciary as the "least dangerous" branch of the government. It has "no direction either of the strength or of the wealth of the society; and can take no active resolution whatever," Hamilton wrote.

In recent terms, however, the Roberts Court has been taking a more assertive stance. Many observers have remarked upon the Court's decisions striking down important government policies ranging from federal campaign finance laws to local school boards' desegregation plans. Although the Court generally grants review to resolve conflicts among the lower courts, it has taken cases involving hot-button issues such as affirmative action even in the absence of disagreement.

A second form of assertiveness has been less noted: the Court is not simply deciding which cases to hear, but is also directing the parties to address issues the justices want to take up and reaching out to decide issues never addressed by the parties.

To be sure, the Court sometimes acts appropriately in raising issues the parties have chosen not to. The 2012 challenge to the individual mandate in the Affordable Health Care Act provides an example. Both the challengers and the federal government wanted the Court to decide the question immediately. But a federal statute (the Anti-Injunction Act) bars courts from entertaining certain kinds of challenges to federal taxes before those taxes have actually been collected. So the justices properly directed the litigants to address whether they had the power to decide the case before the Act came into force. So too with the 2013 challenge to California's marriage restriction. Both the challengers and the private citizens who had sponsored the ballot initiative limiting marriage to opposite-sex couples were hoping for a definitive ruling from the Court on the constitutionality of marriage restrictions, but the Court properly held that that once the state had declined to appeal the trial court's ruling requiring marriage equality, no party had standing to seek further review.

At other times, however, the Court ranges far afield in forcing the parties to address issues they may deliberately have chosen to forgo. And the Roberts

Court has shown a troubling tendency to use this tool to overturn precedent.

The most striking examples involve scheduling cases for re-argument so that the justices can consider issues the parties didn't originally press. Consider *Citizens United v. Federal Election Commission* (2010). A request for re-argument transformed the case from a narrow inquiry into a particular application of the McCain-Feingold campaign finance law into a high-stakes examination of *all* corporate political spending. The Court directed the parties to brief and argue about whether it should overrule its decision in *Austin v. Michigan Chamber of Commerce* (1990), which held that restrictions on campaign spending could be justified by the government's interest in preventing "the corrosive and distorting effects of immense aggregations of wealth that are accumulated with the help of the corporate form and that have little or no correlation to the public's support for the corporation's political ideas." It then issued a bitterly divided 5-4 decision freeing all corporations and unions to use general-treasury funds for any kind of election-related speech and setting the stage for the rise of super PACs. (I discuss the case in more detail earlier, particularly in Chapter 8.)

In the 2012 term, the Court ordered re-argument in another case involving corporate conduct, *Kiobel v. Royal Dutch Petroleum Co.* The plaintiffs in *Kiobel*, former residents of the Ogoni region of Nigeria, claimed that the defendants—including the Shell oil company—provided logistical and financial support to government security forces that engaged in a series of human rights abuses, including extrajudicial killing and torture. The case was brought in the United States under the Alien Tort Statute (ATS), which gives federal district courts jurisdiction over tort claims by aliens for "violation[s] of the law of nations." The ATS was enacted by the first Congress in 1789 and, after lying dormant for the next two centuries, was resurrected in *Filártiga v. Peña-Irala* (1980) to permit foreign victims of particularly egregious and universally condemned human rights abuses to sue the perpetrators in U.S. courts.

The question on which the Supreme Court initially granted review—the question raised by the parties before it—was whether corporations can be sued under the ATS or whether it permits lawsuits only against natural persons. The answer to that question was potentially quite important. The individual corporate employees involved in human rights violations might not themselves be subject to the jurisdiction of U.S. courts, which can adjudicate claims only against defendants who have had sufficient contacts with the United States. So a foreign employee who commits a wrongful act overseas may not be subject to suit here. And even when foreign individuals can be sued in the United States, it may be hard to collect on any judgment. By contrast, it's relatively easy to sue a multinational corporation that also does business domestically, and the company will have assets to satisfy a judgment. (One might be forgiven, in light of the Court's decision in *Citizens United*, for seeing something ironic about the argument that corporations are sufficiently like persons to be entitled to constitutional speech protections while being sufficiently different to avoid liability for human rights violations.)

But the Court upped the ante even further with its order for re-argument. A week after it heard oral argument in the original case, the Court told the parties to file new briefs addressing whether the Alien Tort Statute allows U.S. courts to hear cases "for violations of the law of nations occurring within the territory of a sovereign other than the United States." That order raised the possibility that the Court, beyond shielding foreign corporations from being sued in U.S. courts, would hold that under the ATS *no one* can be sued for human rights violations that occur outside the United States unless they occur on the high seas or in some no man's land. In short, the Court's rewritten question asked whether plaintiffs in *Kiobel* and similar cases can use the ATS to sue torturers who committed their violations on dry land, even if the plaintiffs—as in *Kiobel* itself—or the defendants are now living in the United States. (Disclosure: In *Kiobel*, I submitted amicus briefs on behalf of more than a dozen individual plaintiffs as well as a nonprofit public interest law firm that had brought suits under the ATS against individual human rights violators who had subsequently moved to the United States and were later sued here.)

Chief Justice Roberts's opinion for the Court answered that question by holding that the "presumption against extraterritorial application" governed suits under the ATS. In other words, only if the violation of international law has occurred within the United States or on the high seas will U.S. courts have the power to hear a plaintiff's case. If the violation occurred in another nation's territory, then the ATS provides no basis for U.S. courts to hear the plaintiff's case. In Kiobel's case, Chief Justice Roberts found that "all the relevant conduct took place outside the United States," and thus the presumption against extraterritorial application prevented suit. But the chief justice cautioned that even "where the claims touch and concern the territory of the United States"—as they might when a U.S.-based corporation makes decisions about its activities overseas—they still "must do so with sufficient force to displace the presumption against extraterritorial application."

By contrast, in his concurrence in the judgment, Justice Breyer, joined by Justices Ginsburg, Sotomayor, and Kagan, would have held that the ATS permits U.S. courts to hear cases not only when the alleged violation occurs on American soil, but also when either the defendant is an American national or when "the defendant's conduct substantially and adversely affects an important American national interest," including the interest "in preventing the United States from becoming a safe harbor (free of civil as well as criminal liability) for a torturer or other common enemy of mankind." Justice Breyer's approach would apparently leave open the possibility of ATS lawsuits against individual defendants found in U.S. territory, even if their human rights violations occurred overseas.

PAMELA S. KARLAN   131

The difference in these approaches is hardly academic. Consider the case of Edgegayehu Taye. She was imprisoned and tortured for more than ten months in Ethiopia. The abuse was personally supervised by Kelbessa Negewo, an official of the military dictatorship. After her release, Taye fled to the United States, where she went to work in a hotel in Atlanta. Some years later, she encountered Negewo, who was working in the same hotel. She and other victims filed suit using the ATS, and she obtained a verdict for $200,000 in compensatory damages and $300,000 in punitive damages. Under Chief Justice Roberts's approach, the presumption against extraterritoriality would presumably bar her suit; under Justice Breyer's it clearly would not. In a cryptic concurrence, Justice Kennedy suggested that the chief justice's opinion, which he had joined in full, left open a significant number of questions, but he neither identified those questions, nor suggested how he would answer them.

Kiobel is just one example of the Court dictating which points litigants will argue. The Court used

Kiobel to force a question not presented by the litigants, and the majority made the most of the opportunity, effectively rewriting the existing doctrine. That's a lot of responsibility for an unelected, self-described umpire.

14. Empty Benches

THERE'S A STORY TOLD ABOUT JOE MCCARTHY —not the right-wing senator from Wisconsin, but the manager of the great New York Yankees teams of the 1930s and '40s. McCarthy dreamed that he had died and gone to heaven, where Saint Peter told him to assemble an all-star team. McCarthy was excited: he'd have Christy Mathewson and Walter Johnson, Honus Wagner, Lou Gehrig. Just then, the phone rang. It was Satan challenging McCarthy to a game. "You haven't got a chance of winning," McCarthy exclaimed. "I've got all the players." "Oh, I know that," Satan answered. "But I've got all the umpires."

The umpire can have a huge impact on how the game turns out, as the Supreme Court's self-described umpire-in-chief, John Roberts, has shown. But the chief justice ignores this when he celebrates the fact that today's Court is the first without even a single justice who has served in elective office, claiming that drawing on the lower courts for justices—as opposed to drawing on Congress, governors' offices, and the Cabinet—has shifted the Court from "fluid" considerations of "policy" to the "more solid grounds of legal argument." In the Affordable Care Act cases, where the Court narrowly upheld the individual mandate while imposing new and potentially significant limitations on Congress's commerce and spending clause powers, he wrote that the Justices

> possess neither the expertise nor the prerogative to make policy judgments. Those decisions are entrusted to our nation's elected leaders, who can be thrown out of office if the people disagree with them. It is not our job to protect the people from the consequences of their political choices.

But given how much judges influence policymaking, one of the most important consequences of the people's political choices is the composition of the courts themselves—and not just the Supreme Court. In the 2011 term, the Supreme Court issued opinions in 65 cases after oral argument, the fewest since 1953, when it heard arguments in *Brown v. Board of Education*. Over the past fifteen years, the Court has fairly consistently decided between 75 and 80 cases, roughly half the number it was deciding as recently as the final years of the Burger Court.

At the same time, the federal courts of appeals disposed of more than 57,000 cases in the year ending last September, and the federal district courts of more than 300,000. The judges serving on these lower courts have tremendous leeway on a range of matters, from sentencing individuals in federal criminal cases to determining whether a plaintiff's claim of discrimination is plausible enough to proceed to discovery and trial. Federal laws and policies concerning everything from consumers' rights to privacy to labor protections are enacted by our nation's elected leaders, yet they often are only as effective as the judges who apply them, case by case.

Thus one of the most important legacies a president leaves behind concerns judges who continue to shape the law for decades. Federal judges serve for life, and Justice Stevens's distinguished career—he was nominated by President Gerald Ford and served from 1975 until shortly after his 90th birthday in 2010—is a reminder that judges can live a very long time. In 2012 Judge Wesley Brown, nominated to the federal district court in Wichita, Kansas by President John F. Kennedy in 1962, died while still serving at the age of 104.

The nomination and confirmation process that put Brown on the bench 50 years ago has become increasingly politicized and dysfunctional in the quarter-century since the failed Supreme Court nomination of Robert Bork turned filling the federal bench into a blood sport. Though public attention naturally focuses on Supreme Court seats, much of the real action concerns seats on the thirteen federal courts of appeals and the 94 district courts.

Over the last 30 years, as American politics has become polarized to a degree not seen since the nineteenth century, a conservative legal movement has self-consciously sought to move the federal courts to the right as part of a campaign to roll back key pieces of existing legal doctrine, such as federal power to regulate the environment, broad protections against discrimination, and procedural rights for individuals accused and convicted of crimes. Recent Republican administrations have pursued a judicial nomination strategy that seeks to appoint young, deeply committed conservative lawyers to the federal district courts and courts of appeals. Republican activists pressed judicial nominations as a priority, and conservative presidents and senators worked hard to get these nominees confirmed. The result is not just a deep farm team of potential Supreme Court nominees, but also a host of conservative judges inscribing their views of constitutional law and their interpretations of statutes in thousands of cases that never reach the Supreme Court. If their cases are appealed to the top, then those judges' opinions shape the terms of the debate in the high court.

By contrast, the Obama administration has done relatively little to bring the courts back into balance. When President Obama was sworn into office, there were 55 vacancies on the federal bench. As of March 2013, there were 87, meaning that roughly 10 percent of all judgeships are vacant. Obama is the first president in at least the last few decades "to finish his first term with more vacancies than he inherited," according to Alliance for Justice. (Vacancies weren't tracked before the Reagan years.)

To be sure, much of the problem is conservative obstructionism. Several of the president's most prominent nominees have been filibustered. Many others have been victims of "blue slips"—an internal Senate procedure that allows either senator from a nominee's home state essentially to block a nomination. Even candidates who ultimately are confirmed by overwhelming votes have faced a series of procedural roadblocks. And the prospect of having to put their careers on hold has probably dissuaded many qualified candidates even from seeking nominations.

But conservative obstruction is not the only problem. During the period when Democrats held a filibuster-proof senate, the administration moved far too slowly to make nominations. Granted, it was a busy time, with the economic crisis, two Supreme Court openings, and health care reform occupying the administration's attention. But the delay also reflects a sense that judicial appointments are less important than other policy levers and that the president's base does not really care about the issue.

Moreover, while the current administration has achieved an admirable degree of gender and racial diversity among its picks (nominating roughly two times more women and persons of color, by percentage, than the preceding administration had), its court of appeals nominees are generally older than their conservative counterparts. And very few of them have backgrounds either as public-interest lawyers for liberal or progressive causes or as scholars who have responded to conservative legal thought.

The administration's inability to fill vacant seats on the federal bench has both immediate and long-term effects. Right now, millions of Americans live in jurisdictions facing what the Administrative Office of the U.S. Courts calls "judicial emergencies": their empty benches can't handle heavy caseloads. Because criminal prosecutions take priority, plaintiffs with civil claims—workers, victims of government misconduct, consumers, and others—face severe delays in vindicating their rights.

In the longer term, vacancies accrued during a liberal-leaning administration that remain open for succeeding conservative administrations to fill will ensure that courts continue to skew to the right, meaning that progressive legislation and regulations will be undercut when it comes time to enforce them. The lack of a vigorous judicial response to conservative versions of originalism and "strict construction"—which often means little more than a cramped reading of broadly worded statutes and constitutional provisions—will bias popular discussion and debate.

Even the best players can be hamstrung by a hostile umpire. Unless liberals make sure the umpires are not all from deep right field, they will face serious difficulties down the line.

15. Sometimes an Amendment Is Just an Amendment

THE FOURTEENTH AMENDMENT'S EQUAL PROtection and due process clauses are never far from the news. Last term's federal marriage equality litigation, for example, lay at their intersection. Many transformational events of post-Reconstruction America, from the dismantling of Jim Crow and the protection of reproductive autonomy to the Supreme Court's decision in the 2000 presidential election, would have been impossible without them.

But in recent years two less familiar elements of the amendment—its citizenship clause and its public-debt clause—have taken center stage. Efforts to twist these clauses in the service of policy preferences should remind us that there is a real line between constitutional interpretation and argument in defense of political goals.

One of those efforts concerns birthright citizenship. The first sentence of the first section of the Fourteenth Amendment provides that "all persons born or naturalized in the United States, and subject to the jurisdiction thereof, are citizens of the United States and of the State wherein they reside." This phrase overturned the Supreme Court's notorious *Dred Scott* decision (1857), which held that persons of African descent could never become citizens. When the amendment was ratified in 1868, it conferred citizenship on the newly freed slaves and marked an important turning point in the United States's definition of "We the People."

The language of the citizenship clause is expansive: *all* persons—not just members of a particular race or children of citizens—who are born in the United States are entitled to U.S. citizenship. The qualifying phrase "and subject to the jurisdiction thereof" was included to clarify that children born to foreign diplomats or (perish the thought) foreign invaders occupying U.S. soil would not acquire citizenship.

The authors of the amendment understood the implications of the clause: it would confer citizenship on children of people who were not citizens themselves. For the most part, that posed no problem because the United States then had an open-door policy, at least with respect to most potential immigrants. But the clause applied even to more politically controversial populations. Senator Lyman Trumbull, one of the architects of Reconstruction, responded to criticism that the clause would result in "naturalizing the children of the Chinese and Gypsies born in this country" by affirming that it "undoubtedly" would. And even after Congress passed the first significant restriction on immigration—the Chinese Exclusion Act of 1882—the Supreme Court held in *United States v. Wong Kim Ark* (1898) that a child born within the United States to parents who were ineligible to become citizens nonetheless possessed birthright citizenship.

In recent years, anti-immigration activists have warned of a flood of "anchor babies"—children whose noncitizen mothers travel illegally to the United States to give birth for the purpose not only of obtaining U.S. citizenship for their children but of gaining a pathway to legal residence for themselves as well. Proposals by members of Congress and conservative activists to repeal the citizenship clause in response will surely fail: there is no possibility that they can garner the required two-thirds votes from both houses of Congress. So anti-immigrant activists have turned instead to arguing that the citizenship clause does not mean what it says. They don't deny that their targets were born here. Nor do they deny that those children are subject to the jurisdiction of the United States in the sense that they must obey federal and state law, can be the subject of child-custody or parental-termination decisions by federal or state courts, and so on. But they say that because such children may also owe obedience to their parents' country of citizenship—if that country gives birthright citizenship to children born abroad, which the United States itself does not invariably do, as *Flores-Villar v. United States* (2011) illustrates—they somehow are not sufficiently subject to U.S. jurisdiction to qualify for citizenship because they are not subject exclusively to U.S. jurisdiction.

That position cannot be right. If it were, Congress would also have the power to withhold citizenship to children born in the United States to married couples where one parent holds foreign citizenship. After all, those children might be subject to dual jurisdiction as well. That no one is willing to go that far suggests that the desired policy outcome is driving the interpretation.

Wishful thinking similarly underlies the calls we heard in the summer of 2011 for the president to raise the debt ceiling unilaterally. A federal statute— not the Constitution—limits the amount of debt the federal government can incur. The government hit that limit in the spring, raising the prospect that soon thereafter it would be unable to pay the interest on government debt or spend money on authorized programs. At one point the president and Congress were at a stalemate, with a majority of the House seemingly unwilling to raise the debt ceiling unless they obtained an agreement with regard to the deficit and the federal budget. Some partisans and scholars then turned to section four of the Fourteenth Amendment, which provides, in pertinent part, that "the validity of the public debt of the United States, authorized by law . . . shall not be questioned." These commentators claimed that this provision allowed the president to raise the debt ceiling if doing so was necessary in order to pay the nation's bills.

Ironically, some of the same people urging this unilateral executive action had been suspicious during prior administrations—and even during this one when it came to the president's power to intervene militarily in Libya—of expansive claims of executive power absent congressional authorization. The text of the Constitution cut strongly against them: in the second clause of Article I, section 8, the Constitution expressly confides the power "to borrow Money on the credit of the United States" to Congress, not the president, and section five of the Fourteenth Amendment provides that "Congress"—with no mention of the president—"shall have power to enforce, by appropriate legislation, the provisions of this article." Like the argument over the interpretation of the citizenship clause, the argument here was too clever by half. Not everything on which the federal government is obligated to spend money is a "debt." Nor is failing to pay a bill on time necessarily the same thing as "question[ing]" the underlying debt.

The lesson from these two debates over the meaning of the Fourteenth Amendment's less familiar clauses is sobering: activists, legislators, and scholars alike often are drawn to arguments that serve their politics, but that are more clever than wise.

It was heartening to see many principled conservatives condemn the citizenship clause circumvention and principled liberals reject the public debt clause end run. They remind us that while the Constitution's great clauses are often open texture, they are not empty.

16. It Takes Two

THE SUPREME COURT'S RECENT DECISIONS IN *United States v. Windsor* and *Hollingsworth v. Perry* gave supporters of marriage equality and civil rights for gay Americans much to be thankful for. In *Windsor* the Court struck down the federal Defense of Marriage Act (DOMA), which denied federal benefits to couples validly married under state law. (Disclosure: I represented Edie Windsor, the plaintiff in the DOMA challenge.) And in *Perry* the Court held that proponents of a marriage-restricting initiative lacked standing to appeal a district court ruling striking down the results of the initiative, effectively reinstating marriage equality in California.

These opinions come after years of grassroots advocacy and political action, as well as a carefully constructed litigation campaign, with supporters of marriage equality frequently invoking the Supreme Court's 1967 decision in *Loving v. Virginia* as a guiding star. In that aptly named case, the Court held that Virginia's criminalization of interracial marriage violated two provisions of the Fourteenth Amendment: the equal protection clause, because Virginia's law could be explained only as the product of illegitimate racial prejudice, and the liberty element of the due process clause, because Virginia denied Mildred and Richard Loving "the freedom to marry" that "has long been recognized as one of the vital personal rights essential to the orderly pursuit of happiness by free men." Restricting marriage to opposite-sex couples likewise relies on prejudiced, or empirically dubious, propositions about gay people and their families, and denies them a status that confers dignity and a bundle of tangible entitlements central to modern life.

But even as we embrace *Windsor, Perry, Loving,* and the rights of loving couples, we should remember that it takes much more than a celebrated judicial decision to realize constitutional values.

Loving was the end point of a sustained assault on racial discrimination, and most of the troops in that campaign were not Supreme Court justices. For example, the Court's foundational 1954 decision in *Brown v. Board of Education,* forbidding segregation in public schools, came after President Truman had already issued executive orders ending segregation in the military. When *Brown* reached the Court, President Eisenhower's Department of Justice filed briefs urging the justices to hold racial segregation unconstitutional. And by the time the Court decided *Loving,* the vast majority of states had already repealed laws forbidding interracial marriage. *Loving* was decided a generation after the California Supreme Court, in *Perez v. Sharpe,* had used the Fourteenth Amendment to strike down California's ban on interracial marriage. (In contrast to the California Court, the U.S. Supreme Court disingenuously dodged the marriage issue for a decade, apparently because it feared that a decision striking down bans on interracial marriage would imperil support for *Brown*.)

Rather than anticipating progressive social change, the Supreme Court most often reflects it. The Court did not express serious constitutional skepticism about sex discrimination until 1970, significantly after Congress had enacted the Equal Pay Act and forbidden sex discrimination in employment as part of Title VII of the Civil Rights Act of 1964. Similarly, by the time the Court struck down Texas's sodomy statute in *Lawrence v. Texas* in 2003, most of the states that had at one time criminalized gay sex had abandoned those laws on their own.

Even when the Court articulates constitutional requirements, the active participation of the political branches is needed to meet those requirements. *Brown* was decided in 1954, but in 1964, less than 2 percent of black schoolchildren in the South attended schools with even a single white student. Real desegregation did not begin until the fall of 1969. Why then? Because the federal Department of Health, Education, and Welfare issued guidelines requiring desegregation and threatened to cut off essential federal funds to school systems that did not comply.

How does this history—this interplay between courts and democratic politics—bear on the question of marriage equality? To begin, I cannot think of a contentious social issue on which public opinion has shifted more rapidly. We have moved in roughly a generation from a nation in which no state provided legal recognition to same-sex couples to one in which 30 percent of Americans live in states that provide full marriage equality and another 10 percent live in states that provide legal recognition through civil unions or domestic partnerships. The decisions in *Windsor* and *Perry* came after a historic election in which popular referenda enabled same-sex couples to marry in Maine, Maryland, Minnesota, and Washington State. Congress repealed "Don't Ask Don't Tell," and, as Chief Justice Roberts observed during the oral argument in *Windsor*, "political figures are falling over themselves to endorse" marriage equality. President Obama and Attorney General Eric Holder instructed the federal government's attorneys to argue for DOMA's unconstitutionality, and President Clinton, who signed DOMA into law, urged the Court to strike it down. It seems likely that without these political changes, the Supreme Court would not have been ready to consider legal protections for same-sex couples.

Even with all this change, however, we don't know when the Court will take the final step of holding that the Constitution requires marriage equality. At some point, the Court will almost certainly confront that question: although many states have moved toward marriage equality, 26 states have adopted constitutional amendments to prohibit same-sex marriage, making it unlikely that the political process will produce national uniformity any time soon.

Thus, the marriage cases raise anew the recurring question of when the Court should intervene to declare that a contested social issue has been resolved as a matter of constitutional law. Few institutions are more deeply rooted in the popular consciousness than marriage. That is why marriage always appears—regardless of the justice writing the opinion, from Chief Justice Earl Warren to Chief Justice Rehnquist—in the list of fundamental rights protected by the Constitution. In considering what marriage means today, as it probably will in an upcoming term, the Court will be aiming at a moving target. How the justices answer the marriage question may influence the Court's political and moral capital with future generations in the way that its decisions in cases such as *Loving* did for mine. And so, precisely because feelings about marriage are so fundamental to so many people, there may be two institutions whose futures are on the line: marriage and the Court.

17. The Constitution Without the Court

THE END OF JUNE IS HIGH SEASON AT THE Supreme Court, with the term's final decisions coming down in rapid succession. But then in July and August, the Court recesses. We rarely hear again from the justices until October.

Yet it would be a mistake to think that nothing of constitutional significance happens when the Court is not in session. This past August marked the 50th anniversary of the March on Washington for Jobs and Freedom, an event that has had as great an impact on the development of American constitutional law as any but a handful of Supreme Court decisions.

On August 28, 1963, Dr. Martin Luther King Jr. delivered his "I Have a Dream" speech, asking America to make good on a founding commitment. "When the architects of our republic wrote the magnificent words of the Constitution and the Declaration of Independence," King said, "they were signing a promissory note to which every American was to fall heir": that every person would have an inalienable right to life, liberty, and the pursuit of happiness.

Although King used a legalistic phrase, he and the others who assembled at the Lincoln Memorial had not come to Washington to demand that the judiciary fulfill the Constitution's promise. (John Lewis—the only surviving speaker from the march—had planned to criticize the Kennedy administration for "trying to take the revolution out of the streets and put it into the courts" before he was persuaded to tone down his speech.) Instead the marchers joined together to demand public recognition of black citizens' claims for equality and opportunity, and to pressure

Congress to pass a civil rights bill. Their efforts thus echoed President Franklin Roosevelt's vision of the Constitution as "a layman's document, not a lawyer's contract."

In spite of his reference to the founding documents, King understood that the architects of our republic are not just the 56 men who signed the Declaration of Independence or the 55 men who gathered in Philadelphia for the Constitutional Convention. They include as well the men who crafted the Reconstruction amendments that in many ways marked America's second founding, and ultimately all the men and women who have worked to realize the Constitution's values.

Acutely aware that the Supreme Court had held in the notorious *Dred Scott* decision (1857) that black people "had no rights which the white man was bound to respect" and that Congress lacked the power to ban slavery, the generation that framed the Thirteenth, Fourteenth, and Fifteenth Amendments in the late 1860s created a special role for Congress.

Thus the amendments contain—in addition to their guarantees of freedom, equal protection, and non-discrimination—explicit provisions that Congress may "enforce" the amendments through appropriate legislation. Reflecting Congress's belief that the judiciary could not be relied on to vindicate fully the new constitutional guarantees, Senator Oliver Morton of Indiana explained, "The remedy for the violation of the fourteenth and fifteenth amendments was expressly not left to the courts." The marchers who came to Washington in 1963 demanded that Congress fulfill the constitutional responsibility that Morton and others had left it.

In the year after the March, Congress embarked on what came to be known as the Second Reconstruction: a series of transformative bills that finally began to make good on the promissory note about which King spoke. The Civil Rights Act of 1964 and the Voting Rights Act of 1965, along with executive branch enforcement of statutory provisions, produced real change in people's lives.

These two statutes illustrate how the political branches can use their powers, under both the enforcement clauses of the Reconstruction amendments and the provisions of the original Constitution, to provide a fuller vindication of constitutional values of liberty, equality, and dignity than courts can achieve acting alone.

For example, ten years after the Supreme Court's decision in *Brown v. Board of Education* (1954), less than 3 percent of black schoolchildren in the South had even a single white schoolmate. And nearly a century after the Fifteenth Amendment prohibited denial or abridgement of the right to vote on account of race—and after decades of litigation in which the Supreme Court had condemned violation of the amendment—only 6 percent of black citizens in Mississippi and less than 20 percent of black citizens in Alabama were registered to vote. But once Congress authorized the executive branch to cut off federal funds to school districts that discriminated, real desegregation began in earnest. And when

Congress provided authority for the appointment of federal voting registrars, within five years those officials had enrolled nearly as many black voters in the South as had managed to register in the entire preceding century.

The importance of the political branches in realizing fully the promise of the Constitution—to "establish justice, . . . promote the general welfare, and secure the blessings of liberty to ourselves and our posterity"—stems from the nature of the document. With the exception of the Thirteenth Amendment's ban on slavery, the Constitution's prohibitions and commands operate directly upon the government alone.

In this regard, it is worth considering the Supreme Court's decisions in *Heart of Atlanta Motel v. United States* (1964) and *Katzenbach v. McClung* (1964), which upheld the public accommodations provisions of the Civil Rights Act of 1964—the statute that addressed King's complaint that "we can never be satisfied, as long as our bodies, heavy with the fatigue of travel, cannot gain lodging in the motels of the highways and the hotels of the cities." Quoting the Senate report that accompanied the bill, the Court recognized that "the fundamental object" of the law "was to vindicate 'the deprivation of personal dignity that surely accompanies denials of equal access to public establishments.'" But because private discrimination was at issue, a majority of the Court avoided grounding its decision directly in the Thirteenth and Fourteenth Amendments. Instead the Court welcomed Congress's use of its "ample power" under the Commerce Clause to bar racial discrimination by a wide range of businesses:

> That Congress was legislating against moral wrongs in many of these areas rendered its enactments no less valid. In framing Title II of this Act Congress was also dealing with what it considered a moral problem. But that fact does not detract from the overwhelming evidence of the disruptive effect that racial discrimination has had on commercial intercourse. It was this

burden which empowered Congress to enact appropriate legislation, and, given this basis for the exercise of its power, Congress was not restricted by the fact that the particular obstruction to interstate commerce with which it was dealing was also deemed a moral and social wrong.

In responding to the federal legislative triumphs of the Civil Rights Movement, the Supreme Court did play a role. But that role was to uphold political solutions.

Of course, there are occasions when representative government cannot be trusted, and courts must intervene. In particular, the courts perform an essential function when the group in power has permanently excluded a class of citizens from participating fully in civic life.

But there are other occasions when the political process itself responds actively to the claims of excluded groups or addresses problems that lie beyond what courts are able to fix single-handedly.

In those circumstances—such as during the Second Reconstruction—courts have a special responsibility to support and enforce laws that realize constitutional values of liberty, equality, opportunity, and inclusion more fully than judicial opinions alone can.

Epilogue

A Moveable Court

For liberals and progressives, the end of the 2012–2013 Supreme Court term was the best of times and the worst of times.

Supporters of social equality for gay people experienced a spring of hope and a season of light. The Supreme Court struck down the federal Defense of Marriage Act in *United States v. Windsor* and in *Hollingsworth v. Perry* left in place a district court decision requiring that California restore marriage equality. Within days of the decisions, county clerks in California began issuing marriage licenses to gay and lesbian couples, and the chief administrative officer of the House of Representatives, which had spent millions of taxpayer dollars hiring a high-priced private lawyer to defend DOMA, informed the representatives and their staffs that they would have 60 days to enroll their same-sex spouses in federal benefits programs.

But for supporters of political equality for persons of color, last term marked a winter of despair and a season of darkness. In *Shelby County v. Holder*, the Supreme Court struck down a key provision of the Voting Rights Act and in *Fisher v. University of Texas*, the Court instituted tighter scrutiny for race-conscious admissions policies in higher education. States immediately announced plans to revive restrictive election laws that the Act had previously blocked, including voter ID requirements and redistricting plans that will result in reduced minority voting strength.

The DOMA and Voting Rights Act cases have some important parallels beyond the fact that in both the Court struck down a federal statute. Section 3 of DOMA and Sections 4 and 5 of the Voting Rights Act each involved strong assertions of federal power in areas traditionally left to state regulation. Section 3 of DOMA created, for the first time, a federal definition of marriage. With respect to any of the more than 1,100 federal provisions governing issues from who can be buried in national cemeteries to how political candidates can use campaign funds, DOMA provided that regardless of whether a couple was legally married under state law, "The word 'marriage' means only a legal union between one man and one woman as husband and wife, and the word 'spouse' refers only to a person of the opposite sex who is a husband or a wife." Sections 4 and 5 of the Voting Rights Act created, for the first time, a requirement that certain states and jurisdictions—primarily, but not exclusively, in the South—obtain "preclearance": federal approval before making any changes in their election laws.

Put at a high enough level of abstraction, this federal assertiveness might explain judicial skepticism about each of these laws. As Chief Justice Roberts observed in his opinion in the Affordable

Care Act cases, while "there is a first time for everything," sometimes "the most telling indication of [a] severe constitutional problem . . . is the lack of historical precedent for Congress's action."

But it's important to keep history in mind. The Voting Rights Act came at the end of a century of black disenfranchisement in spite of the requirements of the Fourteenth and Fifteenth Amendments. Finally Congress took its responsibility to enforce those amendments—a responsibility the framers of the amendments deliberately gave to Congress rather than the courts—seriously. Congress's later decisions to extend and amend the Act came after dozens of hearings and were based on thousands of pages of evidence.

By contrast, DOMA was hurriedly passed in 1996 before any state had granted legal recognition to same-sex couples. The "design, purpose, and effect of DOMA," as Justice Kennedy put it, was to undercut state authority not in the service of pursuing a constitutional commitment to equality but in the service of cementing inequality.

So it was especially telling how the Court relied on ideals of equality in the two cases. In *Windsor*, the equality argument was pretty straightforward. New York and other marriage-equality states had decided that same-sex couples were entitled to equality under the law. DOMA denied these legally married couples the tangible equality and the equal status that came along with marriage as a matter of state law. One notable aspect of Justice Kennedy's opinion for the Court was how often it used the word "dignity"—which appears nowhere in the Constitution—to describe the value at stake.

In *Shelby County*, on the other hand, Chief Justice Roberts's opinion for the Court focused not on the value of political equality and dignity for minority citizens, but rather on the claim that the Constitution protects "equality" and "dignity" for the States: by treating states differently, the Voting Rights Act undercut this principle. In reaching that conclusion, the Chief Justice's opinion focused on the framing and on the Tenth Amendment, but ignored entirely the historical context out of which the Fourteenth and Fifteenth Amendments emerged. Americans— and ultimately the courts—must be reminded that the Constitution we have today is not the Constitution of 1789. Even as a pure matter of text, the Constitution today embodies the commitments of the Thirteenth, Fourteenth, and Fifteenth Amendments to racial equality, and the commitments of those amendments plus the Seventeenth, Nineteenth, Twenty Third, Twenty Fourth, and Twenty Sixth to broader political equality.

But neither case was really about technical constitutional doctrine. In *Windsor* Justice Kennedy's opinion never addressed the key doctrinal question of whether discrimination on the basis of sexual orientation should be subject to heightened scrutiny—that is, special judicial skepticism—as distinctions based on race or sex are. Similarly, Chief Justice Roberts's opinion in *Shelby County* never even cites—let alone applies—the existing test for determining when an exercise of congressional power under the Fourteenth

Amendment is "congruent and proportional" to the underlying problem.

Instead the same-sex marriage and voting rights cases are fundamentally about how constitutional principles interact with social conditions. At the oral argument in *Hollingsworth v. Perry*, Justice Scalia demanded to know, "When did it become unconstitutional to exclude homosexual couples from marriage? 1791? 1868, when the Fourteenth Amendment was adopted?" Ted Olson, counsel for Perry, suggested that it became unconstitutional "when we as a culture determined" that sexual orientation should not trigger legal disabilities. Whereupon Justice Scalia asked again, "When did that happen?" When Olson replied, "There's no specific date in time. This is an evolutionary cycle," Justice Scalia shot back, "Well, how am I supposed to know how to decide a case, then, if you can't give me a date when the Constitution changes?"

In one sense, the plaintiff in *Windsor* had a clear-cut answer to that question: DOMA was unconstitutional from the moment it was passed in 1996. The Supreme Court long before had held, "If the constitutional conception of 'equal protection of the laws' means anything, it must, at the very least, mean that a bare congressional desire to harm a politically unpopular group cannot constitute a *legitimate* governmental interest." DOMA clearly flunks that test. But as a matter of legal realism, that answer is unsatisfying. It is very unlikely that the Court would have struck down DOMA in 1996. Society had first to change in ways that affected the justices every bit as much as it affected the two presidents— Clinton and Obama—who came to support marriage equality after their previous reservations.

Justice Scalia and the conservative majority had no trouble relying on their perception of changed social conditions to conduct their constitutional analysis in the *Shelby County* case. Chief Justice Roberts's opinion for the Court held that although the Voting Rights Act had been a constitutionally appropriate response to the world of the 1960s, "Nearly

50 years later, things have changed dramatically." Congress could therefore no longer rely on its understanding of the history, the voluminous evidence before it, and its members' political expertise to conclude that there remained a danger of back-sliding in the states and counties covered by the existing formula. The conservatives brushed aside Justice Ginsburg's insistence in dissent that a primary cause of the change the Court celebrated was the Act itself and that Congress deserved deference when it concluded that "throwing out preclearance when it has worked and is continuing to work to stop discriminatory changes is like throwing away your umbrella in a rainstorm because you are not getting wet."

The real challenge, then, is to understand whether and how the world has changed, and how those changes should inform constitutional interpretation. And here, it seems to me, is where the world outside the courts has most powerfully affected the decisions inside them. The LGBT equality movement has succeeded in the courts because it has managed to gain widespread support from outside the gay community. It has convinced people of good will from across the political spectrum that homophobia exists, that it is wrong, and that constitutional law must respond to gay people's claims for full inclusion in the key institutions of civic life.

By contrast, the civil rights movement, which once seared the nation's conscience and captured its imagination, has lately been far less successful in building a broad popular consensus in favor of racial justice. Perhaps this is because the problems seem so much less tractable; it's far easier to issue marriage licenses than to create good schools for all students. Perhaps this is because distributive justice seems much more a zero-sum game, as people compete for scarce opportunities in higher education and employment. Perhaps this is because increased segregation and income inequality make it far less likely that the powerful feel a connection to excluded minorities: they never wake up to discover that their sons are black and poor.

The Supreme Court seems to think that "there must be some stage in the progress of [the black citizen's] elevation when he takes the rank of a mere citizen, and ceases to be the special favorite of the laws, and when his rights as a citizen, or a man, are to be protected in the ordinary modes by which other men's rights are protected." Those words are from 1883, but they capture perfectly the attitude of the conservatives on the Court today. The irony is that even when minority citizens *do* obtain protection through the "ordinary modes" of politics—as they did by persuading Congress to enact, amend, and extend the Voting Rights Act—the Court steps in to block that progress.

As part of their work, liberals and progressives must rebuild the movement for racial justice so that principles of liberty and equality not only produce legislation that more fully realizes our constitutional commitments, but also create a politics in which the Court too is more fully committed to these ideals.

ABOUT THE AUTHOR

Pamela S. Karlan is Kenneth and Harle Montgomery Professor of Public Interest Law and Co-Director of the Supreme Court Litigation Clinic at Stanford Law School. She has represented parties in more than 50 merits cases before the Supreme Court, arguing seven. After earning her J.D. from Yale Law School, she clerked for Justice Harry Blackmun and served as counsel for the NAACP Legal Defense and Educational Fund. Her column, "Karlan's Court," appears in *Boston Review,* and she is coauthor, with Goodwin Liu and Christopher H. Schroeder, of *Keeping Faith With the Constitution.*

BOSTON REVIEW BOOKS

Boston Review Books is an imprint of *Boston Review*, a bimonthly magazine of ideas. The book series, like the magazine, covers a lot of ground. But a few premises tie it all together: that democracy depends on public discussion; that sometimes understanding means going deep; that vast inequalities are unjust; and that human imagination breaks free from neat political categories. Visit bostonreview.net for more information.